In memory of Dennis

Contents

Exercises

The best way out is always through
Robert Frost

Preface

This book is for the leaving and the left. It is comparatively easy to get a legal divorce; it is not so easy to get an emotional one. This book addresses how to deal with the emotional aspect of your divorce and helps you manage your child's experience of it.

There is no quick fix, no panacea. The impact of divorce needs to be processed, thought about, thought through, so that decisions can be made that will enable healing to take place. I hope the chapters that follow will help you to understand and deal with what is happening to you so that you can work towards a more independent, confident, liberated future.

I have seen the break-up of hundreds of relationships over the last 30 years as a family law barrister representing men and women in their divorce 'battle', and also as a mediator facilitating discussions between separating couples about their finances, their children and themselves. It struck me when I was a barrister that the legal process was not a place where hurt and pain could be understood and healed; so I trained as both a family therapist and a therapist to be able to help people in their struggle to manage the loss of separation. I have set up and run many divorce support groups for individuals feeling alone and isolated and wanting to share their experiences with others and I have given seminars and workshops to countless people who want help to make things better.

It is important to remember that divorce is not only an end, but also a new beginning. It is that sense of a new beginning that I hope to leave you with. By looking at your divorce head on, you will be able to loosen its fearful grip and see how a new start is within your grasp.

What to expect when you are divorcing or separating

We are wholly unprepared for the personal experience of divorce until it happens. Whether we voluntarily embark on the journey of divorce or have it thrust upon us, whether we are young or old, gay or straight, we cannot foresee how deeply it will affect us – how we will be changed as people, forced to face lawyers, court processes, professionals, forms, negotiations and emotional pain of a type never experienced before.

How different is this from other first experiences? When you learn to drive a car, or get a new job, you are not usually catapulted into a whole new world of information and conflicting advice which involve decisions that are crucial to your future. Divorce is a new world, one which seems to have no familiar bearings, a place of bewilderment and confusion.

You may have done the leaving or been left; either way, not only do you have to cope with a torrent of unwelcome emotions, ranging from raw grief through murderous rage to helpless abandonment, you also have to be efficient enough to deal with the practical realities of the separation. Whilst coping with the inability to eat or sleep, concentrate or indeed think, you also have to be clear-headed enough to instruct a solicitor and make sense of your ex-partner's lawyer's letters. At the very moment when the only thing you feel like doing is taking to your bed and never getting up again, some very canny, organised 'you' needs to kick into action.

If you have children, you will need to continue to talk to the person who has hurt you most in the world. You will need to try and be civilised and speak nicely even though you would really like to paint his or her car violet or put a brick through his or her window.

You may need to think for the first time about what you may be entitled to by way of settlement, and about how much you actually spend each month. You may well find yourself wishing you had some clearer idea about your finances, your partner's business dealings and other things that perhaps you depended on your partner for and have not had to worry about for years.

You may feel anxious and fearful about whether you have to move house or area, or start working or change job; and stressed and sad about the fact that if you have children you will not spend every day with them any more. Where will you go on holiday? And who with?

What of your social life? That part of your world which you had happily taken for granted: good friends, social events, holidays and Christmases. You may find yourself removed from the dinner party list (except when required to make up the numbers) and that friends who you thought were 'yours' have turned out to be your ex's and have become part of his or her new life.

Just as you thought the pain couldn't get worse, it can. What you really want is for all your friends to swear an undying allegiance to you and never see your partner again. You want to be included in everything and not made to feel on the outside. Most of all, you would prefer your ex not to have a new partner and not to flaunt that person with absolutely no regard for you.

How hard, then, against this cacophony of emotions and wholesale rearrangement of your way of life, to have to be at your most efficient, your most organised, your most civil and your most motivated. The blow that you have been dealt has practically floored you but you need to appear to be standing and ready.

What will happen?

You may feel all of these things or just some of them. What is sure, though, is that the intensity of all these feelings will ease and gradually fall away. Although it seems to you that you will always feel like this and that it has gone on for ever, you won't and it hasn't.

You will hear friends say that it is time for you to 'move on' or 'get over it'. Do not feel pressurised by this. It is only time when you say it is. You will cry yourself a river until there are no more tears left and one day you will wake up and not want to cry any more. There will come a day when you have a two-minute glimpse of feeling happy, only to have it disappear again. You will have that glimpse again – and this time for longer. You will feel that you have failed and then you won't. You will feel guilty and then you won't and you will feel left out and then you won't. You will see your marriage as so good that you don't know why it needed to end – and then you will slowly see how things were not so good and that you endured a lot.

It is a cliché, but like many 'bons mots' it is true: divorce may be an end but it is also a beginning. It is very frightening having to think about an unplanned future but gradually, as you start to inhabit that future, you will see that there are opportunities that would never have been open to you before. It is a chance to start learning, exploring and developing again – to forge new links and relationships and do some of those things that being in a long-term relationship prevented you from doing.

As a therapist, I can assure you that it is unusual to find someone a few years down the line of divorce or separation who is still in mourning and still full of anger. Just as a fever subsides, so does the intensity of your emotions. People survive. Not just basically but *really*. They develop new relationships, new friends and new joys. They laugh and they make plans.

Will I ever feel better?

Yes. You need to get used to your new status and that doesn't happen overnight. Don't fight your emotions, believing that you shouldn't feel that way. You may not want to feel as upset as you are, but it is completely and utterly normal. Fighting your feelings will just add to your exhaustion. Allow yourself to cry or howl if you want to. It will help you to process what has happened and move through it.

There isn't an emotion that you are feeling, connected with your divorce, that countless others haven't felt too. Don't feel bad about talking about it. Anyone who is shocked or traumatised needs to keep on talking about it until they have talked about it enough. You will know when you have moved through these phases.

Don't be frightened to really look at your situation and explore how you feel. You may need to talk to a professional about it. The more you process it, the quicker will be your recovery. You wouldn't expect someone bereaved to snap out of their grief and nor should you. Nobody ever drowned by wallowing.

You can put a brave face on for the outside world if you are able to or if you feel inclined to, but behind closed doors and with your friends remember that you need to catch up with an event that may have been imposed on you – and catching up takes time. Your partner may seem happy because if he or she has left you they have had much more time to get used to the idea. You will be starting that journey only when you have been left. Catching up is a long-distance run, not a sprint.

There is a lot of advice and information on the net about divorce – plenty to show you that you are one of many who have had this experience. However, your divorce is **yours** and you will be ready to move on from it only when **you** say so.

How to read this book

This book is designed to offer you a calm, therapeutic way to make sense of your feelings – and, if you have children, to help them make sense of theirs too. You can dip in and out of it; you don't need to read it in a linear way, because your feelings aren't linear and some things feel more important on one day and less important on another. As well as information and advice, there are exercises to help you get to where you need to be.

Friendship is born at the moment when one person says to another: What! You too? I thought I was the only one.

C. S. Lewis

What would you like this book to give you?

I would like this book to make you feel that you are not alone, as though, when you read it, you are with a group of other people who are going through, or have been through, similar things to you and that, like them, you are listening to and sharing experiences.

Below is some feedback from people who have attended my workshops and support groups, recounting what it meant to them to hear other people's stories. I hope that by dipping in and out of this book you will be left with similar feelings.

It gave them:

Perspective
Courage
Comfort
A sense of community, of not feeling alone
Hope
Kinship
The idea that things do get better
Relief that others are going through the same thing
Thinking and processing as a good way of distancing
    oneself from raw grief
The confidence that 'I can get through this'

An understanding of a different way to think and feel
The realisation that separation/divorce is a process
    through which one is constantly moving
An ability to think about the positives of severing the
    emotional connection
A realisation that 'I am not unique in all I feel'
The understanding that the process is a dynamic one
And that 'the road is not as long as I thought…'

What you need when you are separated

Do you feel, whether you are newly or perhaps not so newly separated, that your ex has taken your past and your future? If so, like the people who come to my workshops and support groups, you may be looking for some of the following:

Help to calm down
Help to find hope
To find out how to let go
Guidance
To find a way to move on
Help to cope
To manage negative feelings
To feel that you haven't failed
To really believe that there is life after divorce

How long before I get over this divorce?

This is a question I have been asked by almost everyone I have met who is experiencing the pain of separation. They understandably would like to know when they will be able to rid themselves of their heavy burden; and when they will feel more like their old selves.

Unfortunately, there isn't a one-size-fits-all answer.

Some people are able to function reasonably well after a separation and some people aren't. Some people allow the 'story' of their divorce to become their life narrative for many years, telling it as if it was yesterday and letting it inform and explain why life has 'gone wrong': why a job didn't work out, why there hasn't been another relationship, why they have lost their friends or are permanently depressed. To make separation or divorce your life narrative is to be stuck in time and in an event that seems impossible to move beyond.

For some, separation triggers memories of earlier losses that haven't been fully processed and therefore their grief is amplified. It is necessary then to understand those earlier losses and how they are making the present loss seem louder.

For others, the mourning process is successful and

enables them to transfer love, affection and joy for life elsewhere.

You will know where you are on this spectrum and you will be the expert on what feels right and what doesn't.

However, I can say that after a year things should feel better and after two, much better. If after two years the grief, anger and upset feel the same as in the beginning, you may need some professional to help you think about it in a different way.

Overwhelming feelings

'I hate these feelings; I wish they would just go away.'
'Why does he want to move in down the road? It's as if
he *wants* to hurt me further. I'm devastated.'
'Why is she ignoring the impact of her behaviour on
me? She's making me so angry.'
'I had no voice in whether we broke up, she just left.
I feel helpless.'
'He gave me no warning – just said he had had enough.
I feel worthless.'
'I feel like I'm on a rollercoaster.'

Your feelings are entirely normal. You wouldn't be human without them and you are going to harness them and use them to make you stronger. They are not a waste of time; on the contrary, they will help you grow and flourish. Think about times in your life when you were happy – they pass. Think about times in your life when you were unhappy – they pass. Think about times when you were nervous, about an exam or an event – the feelings pass and so will these. When you are suffering and depressed, it is very easy to think that you will always feel like this. You won't. You know that, from thinking about your life and how things change all the time. You are not the person you were 10 or 20 years ago; in a few years' time, you will be different again.

Life and feelings aren't static; they are constantly moving and changing. Take heart from that. Although when you are deep in your pain you won't feel that anything can change, the rational part of you knows that it will. Try to keep hold of that.

What to do

If your feelings overwhelm you, it can be useful to make a list of them. Write them down and then look at them. This will make you feel more in control and in charge of them. You are on the outside looking at them, making some sense of them.

What you write down may surprise you – you may find yourself staring at words expressing feelings that you didn't realise you had, and others that you thought you had moved away from.

It is a bit like taking your temperature when you have a fever. When you confirm your temperature is up, instead of just feeling hot and out of sorts, you know what you are dealing with and understand it better. With understanding comes independence and control. Your feelings will stop running you, and you will know the beginning and the end of them.

Below are just some of the feelings that people who have come to my support groups have written down:

Angry
Abandoned
Lonely
Airbrushed
Jealous
Guilty
Full of shame
Sad
Scared of the future
Disappointed
Stupid
Powerless
Betrayed
Filled with sorrow
Frustrated
Not good enough
Anxious
A failure
Humiliated
Suspicious/unable to trust
Full of rage
Resentful
Out of control

Look at the feelings that you have written down and separate them out in your mind: which ones do you feel more often, and when? Which are the most powerful and make you feel the worst? Which of them only visit from time to time? Notice what sparks one feeling off, and what helps that feeling subside.

One reason I have asked you to make a list of your feelings is to demonstrate that they are containable, and that there is a beginning and an end to them – when you look at them on paper I hope it will help you to feel a little more in control.

Writing your feelings down and sharing them also shows you that you are not alone. These feelings are felt by everyone. You may not feel them all at the same time. Some may be fleeting. The list should make understanding and experiencing them more manageable.

Managing your feelings

In the last chapter, I talked about how important it is to manage overwhelming feelings by thinking about them so that you are more in charge of them and not so much at their mercy. In other words, name them to tame them.

When you are in a calm state, you think first and underneath your thinking is feeling. The thought and the feeling are of equal size. The emotion feels manageable.

When you are in a negative state, the thinking part of you is tiny and the feeling and emotion part of you grows and uses up the thinking space. It feels unmanageable and disconcerting.

In a negative state, you will notice that you are very critical; you reprimand others as well as yourself. You may think, 'Why did I do this?' 'I wish I hadn't said that' or 'I'll never feel better'. You might shout more than usual at a friend or a relative, and your children may be on the receiving end when you feel like this.

When you are in a negative state, *press pause.*

In that moment of pause, connect and start some reflective thinking. 'What am I feeling now?' 'Why am I shouting?' 'Why has everything lost perspective?' 'What has just happened to make me feel like this?'

Try to make the thinking part bigger and the feeling part smaller by explaining what is going on to yourself. See yourself; see the thing that is happening. You will be appealing to the more logical part of yourself.

This doesn't take your feelings away, but it does help to cope with them. You will be much more able to problem-solve, and find solutions. Where there was confusion there will be more clarity.

What lies behind you and what lies in front of you pales in comparison to what lies inside of you.

Ralph Waldo Emerson

Feeling helpless

Do you feel helpless, without power or a voice, unable to function properly, make decisions, think straight or even think at all?

I wonder whether that is because you have projected your ability to manage on to others. You may visit your GP, a neighbour, a friend or a mentor to seek help because you truly believe that you have no capacity inside yourself that you can draw on. You feel you are no good and therefore you take on the mantle of helplessness. Everyone else knows the answers except you.

If you do this, these 'lifelines' that you turn to will go along with it, helpfully giving prescriptions, advice and encouraging words. They may be soothing and go some way to helping you but at the same time their feedback will reinforce your idea that you are hopeless, that you have no resources, that resources somehow belong to others. Everything thus becomes externalised – someone else's thinking and advice – leaving you feeling empty. It keeps you stuck in the not-knowing-can't-do position.

However, being helpless is a myth created by you. You are far from helpless or powerless. Think back to how you were before the separation. You will see that you were totally capable and in charge of decisions and your life. There may be things that your partner did in your division of roles that you have got so used to not doing that you truly believe you can't. All it takes is for you to do those things once or twice and you will quickly realise that you are more than competent. Don't use what you didn't organise in the relationship (planning trips, reading the meter, sorting the Wi-Fi) against yourself. When your partner took on roles so that you didn't have to, you didn't divest yourself of the ability to do those things; you just didn't have to do them, that is all.

You may need to make a sterling effort to reconnect with the resourceful, capable you. Once you take small steps to do this, even if it seems odd at first, it will make you feel so much better. Don't give your strength away – keep it for yourself.

The Attributes exercise at the end of the book will help you with this.

Forwards and backwards

Do you feel like a yoyo? Sometimes you can see tiny green shoots and think that you are on your way; you may have noticed that today was a day when you actually smiled or spontaneously laughed at something. It might be a day when you realise that you have been so involved that a whole minute or hour has passed without you thinking about your divorce or your ex. Then, suddenly you feel that you are back almost at the beginning – plunged back into anxiety and feelings of doom and gloom.

If this is happening to you – you are normal.

The road to recovery isn't a straight line: you don't pass a certain signpost and never see it again. You will travel forwards and backwards time and again, until you notice that the backwards isn't happening quite so much and that the scenery is actually changing.

Be aware of it and clock it – it will make you realise that not only your life is changing, but *you* are changing.

You will not feel like this for ever.

Cry a river until there are no more tears to cry.

Amos Oz

Grief

Breaking up with someone you love can feel like a bereavement. Waves of grief wash over you, sometimes when you are least expecting it, and at times it can feel raw and overwhelming.

Of course it is okay to sob and be overcome with sadness for long periods of time after separation. After all, you are suffering and having to come to terms with the end of something that perhaps you didn't want to finish. Those feelings are normal and you wouldn't be human without them.

Grieving for the end of a relationship sometimes involves grieving for the way you would have liked the relationship to be, for what you *didn't* have, rather than what you did have. Separation can put you in touch with how much you feel you missed out on with your partner, which can make you feel very sad.

Separation grief differs from bereavement. With the death of a loved one, you are 'saying goodbye' to someone who is definitely gone for ever. Bereavement involves coming to terms with that over time and making peace with it.

Separation grief can cause the same sort of feelings but its resolution is complicated because you are mourning the end of a relationship with a person who is still very much around. You are not only reminded of them through others (perhaps your children, or common friends) but often by hearing from or about them or even having to continue to be involved in a dialogue with them.

It is a confusing sort of mourning because it is peppered with so many ambivalent and bewildering feelings that you may have about your ex.

For example you may be full of self-reproach, feel guilty and carry with you a sense of failure. It is a very difficult task to let go of something if you think that you did something wrong and that if you had done things differently maybe you wouldn't have broken up. Your self-incriminating feelings can interfere with the grief process. The 'Feeling stuck' chapter may be helpful to you if this is how you feel.

People grieve in different ways. What feels right for you will inevitably be right for you. It may mean spending time alone, crying. You may want to listen to nostalgic music or have pyjama days. You may surround yourself with people who are supportive and understanding. Grieving is a process, like all aspects of getting over your separation.

If you have been mourning for a long time and you just don't seem to be able to move on, your grief may be mixed up with other feelings with deep roots in earlier experiences. You will need to address that, to distinguish what possibly belongs to earlier losses and what belongs in your break-up.

Just believing that it is okay and natural to grieve can feel like a relief. Grief can be experienced as a cloak which envelops you and which, when you are done with it, you shed to emerge into a new state where you hold the relationship in your memory but you are no longer gripped by it.

Mourning successfully should eventually result in you being able to put the enormity of your pain behind you, to say goodbye to the relationship with sadness and then look forward.

Angry with the world

Most people hate being angry – it is exhausting and seemingly futile. You can't go and put a brick through a window or run someone down, so you are left with a sense of helplessness.

I would say that just because you can't act on your anger doesn't mean that it is pointless. It is a totally legitimate and natural response to trauma and to being treated badly, and an important weapon in the arsenal of weapons needed to get you through your divorce. It is only when you seem to be made up of nothing but anger, and it persists for longer than feels okay, that you may need to do something about it. The 'Letting go of grievance' chapter might be helpful to you if that is the case.

As I said, anger can serve a purpose. It can be a way of dealing with your understandable vulnerability and feelings of fragility. By being contemptuous and scathing of everything and everybody, angry with the world, you do a good job of covering those parts of yourself. No one likes to show or feel weakness. That said, anger can mask things that are important to look at and acknowledge. It can hide those parts of you that you don't want to show even to yourself.

Your anger might make you feel more potent, more in charge, more alive, but if your anger is excessive and you just can't shift it, it is likely to be hiding more frightening feelings, and it can be useful to think about what these are.

What would happen if you let some of it go? Do you feel you might collapse, disintegrate or become depressed? Often this is a fear rather than the reality. Anger is also a very effective distraction from reclaiming your life.

If you have given it some consideration and you believe you have reason to be worried, then seeing a counsellor to help you work through these things and dismantle some of your hostility is a good thing to do. There is no need to white-knuckle anything. There is no harm or stigma attached to asking for help when you need it.

If you can see what your anger is doing, and are able to get in touch with the more frightened parts of yourself, your feelings will be less overwhelming and exhausting and this in turn will enable you to give people a chance to get close to you and help you.

Anger does the very thing that you would rather it didn't. It can make friends or family feel they are treading on egg shells and make them give you a wide berth. It pushes them away at a time when you are longing for closeness and connection. The more they respond to your anger by keeping their distance the angrier you become.

In summary:

- Anger is important and necessary.
- Watch when it goes on for too long and seems to be contributing to you feeling stuck.
- Notice whether it is a way of masking more vulnerable aspects of yourself. Is it more comfortable to feel angry than to feel sad?
- You may be pushing people away with your anger when you need them to support you and be close to you.

Loss

Most people who have not experienced separation imagine that what is involved is simply the loss of a relationship, a partner. However, the sense of loss is often much broader and less defined than that. Divorce support group members in workshops I have run listed the following as some of the losses that come with separation:

Friends
Confidence
Dreams
Plans
Vision
Family
In-laws
Home
Faith in new relationships
Lifestyle
Wealth
Material possessions
Position
Status
Identity

Security – emotional and financial
Intimacy
Companionship
Planned-for future
Hope
Self-esteem

Separation and divorce accentuate loss on all sorts of levels – and are deeply disruptive. It is important to manage the sense of loss in the right way.

Rita came to one of the divorce support groups that I ran. There were nine people in the group, made up of five women and four men. Rita was 15 months into her break-up. She was 39 and had lived with her partner for 12 years. She felt numb and said that she found it difficult to eat and had no appetite. She had lost 7kg. She was very thin and the group were worried about her. The loss of her partner had been so disruptive to her life that she was missing not only him, but also the idea of a baby that they had been trying to conceive when he left. Rita said she didn't want to eat because what was the point? She said, 'He clearly didn't find me attractive enough to want to stay with me, so I don't care about myself any more. I have lost having children now too.' What she had lost was any idea that life goes on and she was punishing herself by not eating and giving up on ever having children. She had experienced her ex leaving as persecuting and had continued to persecute herself long after he had gone by not really living. The world felt empty for her, and in the aftermath of their break-up she wasn't able to see that the world still existed and all her qualities and many positive aspects of her life were still there. Another group member said to her, 'It is like you have put yourself in a dark room and forgotten that if you open the curtains the light comes in.' She replied, 'I don't want to open the curtains.'

It is important to recognise when feelings of loss convert to depression. Rita had become depressed, which meant that she had no energy for life. The support group helped her get in touch with her whole self, not only the depressed part, but also the very alive part. She had a job, she had friends she had lost touch with, and she had a family. She had unconsciously chosen to keep herself where her ex had put her because she bought into the idea that that was where she belonged. The group helped her see that she could start living again. They talked about her not needing to psychologically stay where he left her; that it was her life and she could now choose to live it. Gradually, over the weeks, she started to engage more and reignite her interest in life.

When you have had a shock, or are very badly hurt, it's not unusual to find it really difficult to eat, and to feel that you can't take in anything that might nourish you. Your aversion to food is linked to keeping yourself depleted – you don't feel you are deserving of taking in any goodness, or anything that would make you feel better, or whole. However, you don't need to keep yourself short. As your self-esteem grows, and you start to feel worthy of taking in good experiences again, you will find your appetite coming back.

It is important to recognise that although your loss is real, it isn't the whole picture. As soon as you feel engulfed by loss, try to spend some time thinking about the parts of your life that are still intact. That is not to say 'count your blessings', which you may think is unhelpful, but to try to hold on to the wider perspective, which will definitely be there if you think about it.

What does an ending look like?

Often there is lack of clarity about what the ending of a relationship looks like. On one level you understand that you or your partner has left for whatever reasons, but what then? How do you move from being part of a couple to severing that connection and feeling separate? The word 'separated' is a label that describes your new situation but it may not be how you feel.

A relationship doesn't just end because you make that decision or because you physically separate. It ends when you emotionally separate.

The ending of a relationship is a process, but if you or your friends would describe you, months or years on, as still involved in some way, then perhaps the enemy is not your ex, but the self-imposed constraints and restrictions that are holding you back, keeping you in a state of limbo, and stopping you from enjoying a fully lived life.

The ending should look exactly like that after a while – i.e. an end which is evidenced by your new life that closes the gap on your past and replaces the relationship with anything else that satisfies you.

Looking back through rose-tinted glasses

Jim's wife had left him. He talked about her with love and tears and told me how wonderful she was. He said he was devastated. He couldn't understand at all why she had left and why she didn't want to make any attempt at reconciliation. He told me that their 10-year relationship had been incredible, and how happy they had been together.

I was curious about the mismatch between this utopian description of a relationship and the fact that his wife had walked out on him. She couldn't have shared his view. I asked him to tell me about their relationship, what it was like. He said: 'Well, we were very happy, we didn't spend much time together because I travelled for work and was away for two weeks every month. When I got back, I had to make sure my parents were okay and spent some of each weekend with them. Julie didn't mind at all. She was wonderful; she never complained about anything.'

I asked him what they did together.

'Together? Well, not much but then we knew that one day we would have more time to spend with each other. She really understood that I didn't want to make love more than once a month because I was so tired.'

What was clearly emerging was that Jim was living in a land not occupied by his wife. A land in which he had painted a picture of bliss and the reality was in fact something different.

There was also something cut off about Jim's experience of his marriage. What he described was less than ideal, and his refusal to see this seemed blinkered and bordering on illogical.

In my experience, many people who have been left have a firm belief that the relationship was something that it wasn't. They gloss over the cracks and in so doing miss something. It is often only after some deep exploration of the reality of the relationship that a more complex and true picture emerges.

You may be looking back with rose-tinted spectacles at what you had, but if you spend some time really thinking about what you felt about your partner and your everyday life, a new picture might emerge. We lose track quite easily of what things were really like.

Many people tell what seems to be an idyllic story of a relationship, only to reveal, when their experience is challenged, that things were not quite so. It is helpful to sit down and work out what the relationship was really like. If necessary, ask friends to remind you of what you used to complain about or how the relationship seemed to them.

Jim wasn't only duping himself but doing himself out of something that he needed – a deep emotional connection. He and his wife had colluded with each other to avoid having a close relationship. Julie colluded by not complaining or communicating how she felt and Jim colluded by convincing himself that the lack of connection was not a problem.

Getting in touch with a more complex, detailed picture of the relationship can help you begin to cope with the separation. Rather than hold on to an idyll which would be very hard to break away from, try to inject a dose of truth into the memory of the relationship so that you won't feel quite so let down.

It seems that Julie had missed out on getting what she needed from Jim and had chosen to leave. Jim, in pretending that everything was okay, had denied himself a meaningful relationship and, importantly, prevented himself from understanding why the relationship was over and therefore stopped himself from letting go.

After separation, it can be disturbing to have continued feelings of attachment and nostalgic thoughts of the nearly 'ideal' relationship which you yearn for. Gathering evidence of the nuts and bolts of the relationship will help you to see it for what it was and realise that it is not such a mystery that it fell apart.

I was always looking outside myself for strength and confidence but it comes from within. It is there all the time.

Anna Freud

Loneliness

Many people who come to my support groups talk about how lonely they felt in their marriages. You don't have to live on your own to feel lonely; you can be surrounded by people and still feel it. Perhaps you were lonely in your marriage because you felt invisible and unappreciated.

If you feel lonely once you have broken up, try to get back in touch with people that you have lost contact with. Many people talk about how they let friendships and interests drift. Loneliness is transitory; it comes and goes. You are more prone to feel it when you are at a loose end. Make sure you have enough contact and structure in your week to keep you occupied. At first this might feel like a real effort but it will come naturally to you soon enough. Try and hitch up with people either in similar circumstances or who share an interest or hobby with you.

Sometimes you feel lonely because deep down you are not sure that you are interesting or have anything to offer, so life seems a bit drab. You then feel cut off and alone. You feel alone with yourself. It is coming from within you.

You may have stored the separation in your mind as

a failure to relate. This may get in the way of you making connections with people, friends who want to support you, and so compound the sense of isolation.

Whilst it is understandable for you to feel like that when you have had such a huge knock to your self-esteem, give some thought to what you do have to offer. In other words, make a deep connection with yourself – you may be very pleasantly surprised. The more you like yourself, the more you will attract the good things that you need in your life. If you have been left or have left someone because you were unhappy, you are likely to feel about yourself what your ex has made you feel. Look at yourself with fresh eyes. Are you dull or bad company or unlovable? I am pretty sure that is not the case. If you think it is, you are simply reflecting back to yourself your experience of what is was like to be with someone who didn't take a deep and loving interest in you. Consequently you don't take a deep interest in yourself and that will make you feel lonely.

Do the Attributes, Self-esteem and Who am I exercises at the back of this book to start to get to know again the interesting, creative, joyful you who is still very much there. It will be a good way of mitigating some of the feelings of being alone. If you can be with yourself because you like yourself, you will feel a whole lot less lonely.

The secret of change is to focus all your energy, not on fighting the old, but on building the new.

Socrates

Feeling stuck

Many people feel 'stuck,' unable to get past the ending of their relationship even though they are separated and perhaps even divorced. You may feel that you just can't move away from the emotional pull of it. You are preoccupied with thoughts of your ex, what he or she is doing. You may be annoyed that he or she brought the children back late, or that maintenance is two days overdue, or be agitated that a friend has reported seeing him or her in the pub.

You may constantly check to see if your ex is online and then spend time imagining what he or she is doing, and who with.

You may conjure up a million and one reasons to think about your ex, which all serve to prevent you from letting go. It is exhausting and feels unsatisfactory.

Janie had been separated from her husband for two years. She felt embarrassed that she could not seem to move on. She said that she was sad a lot of the time; she felt angry with herself and couldn't understand why, when her friends were telling her that it was time to let go, she just couldn't. She told me that her mother-in-law, with whom she had had a great relationship, supported her ex, often telling her how wonderful he was, which made her feel worse. She said that even after all this time she missed him. She knew that there was no chance of getting back together because he was with someone else. Nevertheless, she said that whenever she had to see him, she would make an effort to look nice, just in case he changed his mind. She told me that during the relationship she wasn't that happy, as he often criticised the way she did things, making her feel that she wasn't doing enough for him. Janie often belittled herself, saying things like 'I am not very good at that' or 'I don't think I'm good at my job'.

Everything that Janie told me was about her history with her ex. Even though two years had passed, she told me nothing that involved her thinking about anything in the future and there was not much about the present. It felt as if her relationship was in a time warp, stuck in the past, and her loyalty was to that part of her life.

When I asked Janie about any plans she may have, she said she didn't want to make any. She said that there was one part of her that actually didn't want to move on. She agreed when friends said she should, but what she really thought was that she shouldn't. It seemed to me that she was reliving experiences in the past as a way of defending herself against the reality of the ending of the relationship.

With endings come loss and with loss come fear and grief. Little wonder that endings are so difficult to bear.

If you are to face it being over, you have to think about the here and now and the future. Sometimes the future can look like a vast uninhabitable space, one too frightening to contemplate. The past is painful but the future may feel unbearable, so it can seem to you that being stuck in the past is the lesser of two evils.

Janie's way of defending herself from the reality of her relationship being over was to dwell in a land of self-recrimination. She took to heart all her ex's cruel criticisms of her and used them to continue to attack herself in his absence. Living with this constant emotional self-beating was so occupying that it kept her distracted from dealing with her break-up.

Self-criticism and thinking harshly about herself conjured up for Janie how she had felt when she was in the relationship, so she could maintain a fiction of still being in it because it didn't feel much different.

Her guilty belief that she was implicated in the reasons why he left her maintained her connectedness with her ex and prevented her from being free of him. She carried him with her in her mind. To begin to let go, Janie needed to understand that his emotional abuse of her and cruel remarks were not her fault. She had not asked for them or deserved them. She could therefore begin to feel less guilty and so free herself. Janie started to recognise not only that her guilty feelings put a brake on her living her life, but also that she had been unknowingly using them to stop herself facing forwards. By doing so, she was not giving herself the chance she deserved.

There are many ways of recruiting feelings to avoid facing the ending. Janie's was one of them. Sometimes it's holding onto grievances and anger, locking yourself into a cycle of frustrated connection with your ex. Sometimes it's the fear of an unknown future. Sometimes it's the belief that you just can't manage on your own, having been so used to decisions and plans being made for you.

Manuel, who had been coming to our group support sessions, said:

'I have thought and talked about her more in the last six months than I ever did in the last 26 years.'

What to do

Being aware of how your thinking patterns prevent you from moving on is a first step towards knowing that it is your way of not fully accepting the loss.

Try and notice that when you are 'torturing' yourself with thoughts of your ex, you are staying with the familiar and not facing the unfamiliar. This keeps you stuck.

Write down some of your thoughts about letting your relationship go. Read them back from time to time, and think about what it would feel like to cut that chord with your ex.

Make notes about how you think you would feel if you severed the emotional connection and add to them, over a period of days.

This is a list of what some of our group members thought were the benefits of letting go of the cycle of restrictive thinking. They thought it would make them feel:

Free
Energised
Creative
Less claustrophobic
Excited
Relieved
No longer anxious
Empowered
Kinder to others
Wise

Finally, write down one thing that you could do which would signify something different for you and show a break, however small, from the past. One thing that would let you know that you are spending just a little time looking forward rather than looking back.

Remind yourself that divorce is not only an end, but the beginning of a new chapter in your life. Beginnings have ends and ends have beginnings too...

Holding onto a grievance or resentment is like drinking poison and thinking it will kill your enemy.

Nelson Mandela

Letting go of grievance

Grievance plays an important part in the story of separation. You may feel provoked, irritated, annoyed and downright angry with your ex. You may get provocative texts or emails from him or her that make you see red, or you may be sending reasonable requests or messages only to be met with no response at all. It is hard to manage some of those feelings and all you may wish for is some peace.

You may well have legitimate grievances against your ex, perhaps because your divorce isn't concluded or because you need to make childcare arrangements and there seems to be little cooperation over them. Many a hurt feeling is played out in the divorce process, with both parties using every opportunity to score points. It can feel similar to the bickering that goes on between siblings. You might find it hard to control yourself when faced with some off-the-cuff remark aimed at riling you, which sometimes hits the target and provokes you to make your raw feelings known. It doesn't make you feel better, though. You are just left with a pounding heart. Sometimes there is nothing more enraging than feeling that what you say and what you want have no impact on your ex. In fact, the more you communicate a desired outcome, the less likely it seems that you will get it. The problem is, when the process of separation is long and drawn out and opportunities to settle differences are not taken, the legal separation can be unnecessarily prolonged.

It may be that you are holding on to grievances as a way of avoiding the finality of separation. Jo had spent years battling through her divorce and it was still ongoing. Every week she would arrive in the consulting room with a catalogue of what her ex had said and done or not said and done in the last few days. They had been within inches of settling their marital finances several times, and each time, one of them had pulled out on a point of principle. Jo was beside herself; she would rail about his lack of consideration and say she would not give in. There were some loose ends that they could not agree on and she was not going to compromise further. To her mind, he had not suffered as much as she had, so why should she make things any easier for him? Not giving in was both financially and emotionally costly but her rage towards him would not allow her to look at it all with a cool head.

So what was going on with Jo? Why would a divorce take years? Jo's ex was certainly uncooperative and unhelpful, but she would polarise herself and there-fore him by not missing an opportunity to take up arms against him. Whenever we talked about their situation and whether in fact she found the idea of separation so unbearable that she had to keep this going on indefi-nitely, she would collapse in tears. The pain of holding onto grievance was easier than being alone and truly separated.

It seemed that for Jo, the fear of the separation was much worse than the separation itself. Jo was simply exhausted from the battle and from 'measuring' everything that her ex was doing. She needed to let go of it for her own sanity. When he provoked her, she needed to respond calmly, to stop standing on principle and work out – with a clear head – what was best for her and their child, even if it meant giving up on some things. She needed to reclaim her life and to stop engaging in the displacement activity of sustaining her grievances. She needed to start to look at her future without him in it – to face her fear of looking forwards.

How to release yourself from grievance:

- Be conscious of it. Notice when you are complaining about your ex and try and stop yourself. Remember the complaint doesn't change anything; it just keeps you invested in an unsatisfying dynamic.
- The more you stop yourself complaining, the more you will realise how much there is out there for you that you have been too distracted to see.
- Be aware of how the complaint holds you back. Watch how it makes you feel you are involved in the 'myth' of still being in a couple. It also stops you mourning the loss of your relationship and keeps you stuck in the past.
- Have a 'day off' from airing grievances and see how

that makes you feel. Then increase the time to two days and so on.

Trust

Sabrina found out that her husband had been sleeping with someone else when a letter addressed to her arrived. It said, 'I just want you to know that your husband has been having an affair for the last three years. Everyone knows, I thought you should.' It was anonymous.

Finola was suspicious about a work relationship that her husband had, but he denied it was anything but professional. One day she opened the front door to a man she had never met. He told her that his wife was sleeping with her husband. Finola felt that her world collapsed in that moment.

People find out about their partners' infidelities in many ways – by seeing text messages or emails ('can't wait to see you xx'), overhearing phone conversations, finding receipts for dinners or hotels carelessly left in pockets. Discovery can feel like a seismic shock and everything that you have believed in seems to crumble in a flash.

Betrayal goes to the core of your being. Without fidelity, the relationship is stripped of its meaning and of the basic tenet which holds it together. Discovering infidelity is so deeply painful and shocking that it can take a long time to recover from it. Discovery is just the beginning. It raises more questions than it answers. Why, how, when, where, how often are just some of the questions, and if answers are forthcoming, they lead to even more questions.

What do we do with betrayal? Does it always signal the end, or is it the start of communication that can lead to a more meaningful relationship? Sometimes the person having the affair doesn't want to give it up and uses it as a reason to leave. You may feel a primal pain of abandonment, and feel that trust in anything seems impossible. Betrayal makes a mockery of everything you have experienced and shared.

So what next? Where do you go from there? You may be a long way off from this, but there will come a time when you feel that you are getting over both the betrayal *and* your separation. You may be starting to think about dating or people may be 'helpfully' trying to set you up or make suggestions regarding how you could meet someone. And while part of you likes the idea of it, another part thinks it is impossible to trust again and all the doubts come flooding back.

What to do

It may sound strange but really the only way you can find out if you can trust someone is to trust them. It will involve taking a risk; it will involve making your fragile and understandably cautious feelings vulnerable to hurt.

It may *feel* impossible, but it isn't. The human spirit has hope if nothing else.

Looking back, you may realise that bringing up children or the busyness of your everyday life distracted you from seeing that your partner was straying. Or you might have guessed but turned a blind eye in the hope it was not a reality. Second time around, you will be more alert to things not quite fitting together; you will have more sensitive antennae to be able to protect yourself better. If you are vigilant and listen to what your gut tells you about someone, you will make sensible choices.

By avoiding forming new relationships, you will be protecting yourself from betrayal, which is a good thing but, if you are fundamentally a relationship person, this is a high price to pay. So much of what we do in life entails risk. To take a risk, albeit a calculated one, is to live a life and not hide away.

Telling your children

A family changed, not a family broken

These questions may be worrying you:

- How should I tell them?
- When is it best to tell them?
- What should I tell them?

You might feel that once a decision to separate has been made you need to tell the children immediately, before really working out what the separation will look like. Alternatively, you may feel a complete lack of desire to tell the children and that may be a way of avoiding the fact that your relationship is ending and helping you stay in the no-man's land of the status quo.

You will, of course, need to tell the children if the separation is going to happen.

It is important to anticipate what some of the questions will be and to have answers for them. Depending on their age, some children will want to know who they will be living with, when they will see their other parent, whether they are moving house and understandably, why their parents are separating. You may not have all the answers to these questions immediately but so long as you are still living under the same roof as your soon-to-be ex, you have some time to create a framework within which you can talk to your children.

How to do it

Firstly, talk with your ex about what you are both going to say. This can be particularly painful, especially when the decision to separate isn't a mutual one.

It will be tempting to let your children know what one of their parents has done wrong. It may feel like a relief to inform them that their parent isn't as ideal as they might have thought he or she was. However, that information won't help them; it will only serve to hinder their development. What may be a relief for you would in fact be the opposite for them.

Chandrika, in one of my groups, said, 'I am not going to be implicated in the break-up of our family, when it wasn't my decision. I don't want him telling them that "we have decided to separate". We haven't. He has decided it.'

That is understandable anger talking, but it doesn't help your children.

In an ideal world, talking to your children together would be good but it is also fine if that isn't possible, because other things, including how you say it, are more important.

In any separation, the two partners' stories are almost never the same. Try to co-create a non-blaming story that, despite your anger or upset, you can present to your children so that they do not hear conflicting accounts and perceptions. Conflicting accounts are a way of unwittingly inviting your children to stand in judgement, which is not really the job of a child of any age. If you can't agree a script, then the next best thing is for you each to tell them your own version separately.

If you point the finger, your children will feel badly about that parent which will inhibit their relationship with him or her and they will immediately 'side' with you to protect you. Although this may feel nice and supportive, it is not good for them (there is more about this in the 'Managing the relationship with your ex' chapter).

You will need to bite your tongue when your children recount to you what your ex is telling them, even though you know that it is clearly wrong and you understandably want to put the record straight. You may feel that you are a good contender for an Oscar by doing what is best whilst feeling something akin to murderous.

If your ex won't listen to you and tells a different story, you have no choice but to accept that his or her version is different and tell your children that you see what has happened a little differently, but that's fine. Tell them that whatever the truth is, it is between their parents and not for them to make sense of.

What matters most is that you are there as parents to them whatever is going on between the two of you as adults. It is better for them to hold two versions and see that you can too, and that neither of you are recruiting them to your world view.

When to tell them

Once you have broadly worked out what your separation is going to look like, find a time for you all to sit down together. It is always better to make sure that it's not a Sunday evening before the start of the school week, or the day before a birthday or special event, or before important exams.

Try and find a time that has some space around it for managing any consequences – so your children can process what has been said and you can be around to answer any questions.

If you or your partner plan to move out, it is best to tell them one or two weeks beforehand so that they can get used to the idea. They may then be part of the process: go to see where the new home is, and think about how their bedrooms will look. It might be difficult for them to manage if you tell them one day and are moving out the next.

If one of you has already moved out under the guise of being away for work or some another reason, then initially it will not seem like a major change.

Some people have already organised relatively separate lives prior to officially separating; for example having the children on alternate weekends, so some aspects of the separation might feel quite familiar already.

All families are different so there is no fixed rule but there are helpful guidelines. You will be an expert on what you feel is best for your child and you will be acting in good faith for their benefit.

What to tell them

Depending on their ages, your children may already have a pretty good idea that things aren't great and so it may not come as a total surprise. If you have already been living semi-separate lives for a while, or if they have heard you arguing or seen you sleep in different rooms, what you tell them may not be entirely unexpected.

If the separation was a shock for you, then the chances are it will be for your children too. This will make things harder and you will need to choose your words carefully.

Children are mainly preoccupied with preserving their own relationship with both parents and their primary anxiety will be the impact on them, how different will their lives be, what the separation will mean in real terms to them on an everyday basis. How often will they see their other parent? If one of their parents is moving out, are they being left, abandoned, or will their own relationship remain intact? Their other preoccupation is your survival.

You will obviously have to pitch your language appropriately, but whether your children are two or 18, there are three important pieces of information that they need to know:

- That you are separating from each other and not from them. You will need to give some reasons, such as you don't get on well enough to stay together, or you don't make each other happy like you used to.
- That your love for them is constant and that sort of love doesn't change.
- That their home is with both of you even if it is in different places.

One of our group members told his children:

> 'Mum and Dad don't want to be a husband and wife any more but we still want to be a Mum and Dad so...'

It is also really important to tell them that you are there to answer any questions that they might have even if they can't think of any right now. Let them know the plans as far as you know them, such as who is going to fetch them from school, if the routine will change and how weekends will look going forward. Let them know that you are a family changed, not a family broken; and that you and their other parent will continue to parent them together and make decisions together for their benefit.

All they want to know is that they will be okay and that you will survive. There is more on this in the 'Some words to tell the children' chapter.

Some of the questions that you may get are: 'Don't you love Mummy/Daddy any more?' 'Why can't you live together any more?' 'What has happened?' 'Has Mummy/Daddy been horrible to you?' Whatever question they ask, the answers you give must be consistent, along the lines of: 'Adult/grown-up relationships are complicated but what has gone on is private and between us.' If there is a third party involved, painful as it may be, you need to say at some point: 'Yes, Daddy/Mummy has met someone else.' If you are pressed to give reasons, although it may not sit well with you, the best thing to say is 'The reasons are between us' or 'Mummy/Daddy will be happy with X and I want her/him to be happy and I will be too.' Unless there is a pressing reason to do so, it may not be necessary to talk about the third party *at the very beginning.*

It is an impossible task to hide just how sad and upset you are from sensitive and intuitive children, but you will have to contain something of it so that there is space for them to have their own experience of it. If asked, you can say you feel sad but things will get better.

How one couple explained things to their children

Rick and Soraya had agreed after 30 years together to separate. It was no longer working and although they had a lot of respect for each other, they both knew they wanted out. They were upset and anxious and the anger with each other for the disappointments of the marriage was bubbling just below the surface.

They wanted help with what to tell their daughter and two sons who were aged between 21 and 28. They were a family who had a long history of spending time together, meeting up for Sunday lunch and going on holiday once a year, not only with their children's partners but also with family friends who had known them for the length of their marriage.

Their anxiety was due to the fact that apart from a couple of close trusted friends, no one knew they felt like this and they wondered how they could manage any anticipated fall-out. They were beside themselves with worry about how the children would react. Would they be angry that they had no idea that their parents' marriage had 'died' many years earlier? Would they think that all the nice times they had had together over the years had been a sham?

They wanted to deliver a message that their children would understand and that could also be used to explain the situation to close family friends.

This took some thinking. Their main concern was that the children, whom they had always supported together, would have no idea and therefore be very shocked. They were tearful when they talked about what it might do to their children.

We talked for a long time about the children and what stage of life they were at. One had just left college and was still living at home, the oldest was working and living with a long-term partner and the middle child, living in a flat share, was also working and had just finished with his girlfriend. As Rick and Soraya talked about their children, it became clear that the older two were pretty much launched into their own independent worlds. They had friends, work and a good relationship with each other. The youngest was on his way to being independent.

They wanted to rehearse exactly what to say and when to say it. They wanted to talk through the questions the children would have and how they would answer them.

Every time they got close to discussing what to say to their children, their anger at each other flared up. Although it was clear they had a friendship, there was a part of each of them that blamed the other for getting to this point. They were both hurt at having to deal with the separation at this stage of their lives.

As they spoke, however, it also became clear that their separation was going to give them the possibility of something else in life. By separating amicably, they were supporting each other to find a future that had the potential to make each of them much happier than they had been for many years.

I was struck by the rehearsal of grievance, despite their assurances that the split was mutual. We talked this through.

They began to understand that what was being played out in the consulting room was what had been played out between them for years, which meant that they might physically separate but be locked in a dance of mutual recrimination, keeping them emotionally connected for a long time to come. This was what was getting in the way of deciding what to tell their children because, whenever they came to the point of explanation, the dance of anger and blame began again.

Rick and Soraya really began to understand that this was keeping them emotionally connected in a destructive way. I invited them to think about their long marriage in a different way, not denying them their frustrations and hurt but thinking about what they had together which their children would remember. They talked about the fun times they had had together as a family, how the children came to them in different ways for advice and how they had supported them as a team, always being there for them.

When they spoke like this, they saw that *for the children* they had been good parents and had provided something solid and reliable for them, out of which they could launch themselves successfully as adults.

What was important was that, through thinking and talking, they could see that their relationship with each other and its complications were not the children's business. That aspect was something that they needed to deal with themselves.

They were then able to concentrate on what they would actually say.

I asked them what they wanted to communicate. They made a list:

- That they were still a family and would always be.
- That both had felt for some time that their relationship as a couple had run its course and they were friends but it felt inauthentic to stay married.
- That they understood that it might be a shock for the children but the children would see as things unfolded that their relationships with each of them would stay absolutely the same.
- That family events such as weddings, or religious celebrations would involve them all being together.
- That they would live separately and that home was wherever they wanted to come to – it was not either Rick's new flat or Soraya's new flat but both.
- That the children weren't losing them as parents.
- That they would be happier apart than together and that they both wanted it.
- They also decided that, if or when the children asked why they had stayed together for years if they weren't happy, rather than saying 'for you', which would perhaps make them feel responsible

for their parents' unhappiness, they would say they had wanted to, despite their difficulties, but that after much talking this now felt like the right time to separate.

Some words to tell your children

Children don't need to be told the details of your relationship. The whole truth can be a blunt instrument. In fact, the truth is frequently used as a way of exacting revenge. It is often better not to tell the whole truth in the interests of preserving your children's relationship with their other parent.

If one parent has left for another relationship, the following words cover it without drawing the children into being judge and jury:

- Love changes.
- Mum and Dad want different things.
- Both of us love you.
- We are separating from each other not from you.
- We've had problems that we've not been able to work out.
- We are here to answer any questions you may have.

How to tell your friends and family

Telling your family and friends that you are separating can be almost as difficult as telling your children. The chances are that some close family members and friends will already know because you will have confided in them, but what about your wider social circle and all the other people involved in your lives?

Fiona and Rakesh decided there was no life left in their marriage. They wanted to find a way to tell people without, as Fiona said, 'telling individuals one by one as each of us happen to bump into people'. She said that what she wouldn't be able to bear were people's responses as she told them in the street or wherever she happened to see them. Rakesh didn't want the 'look of sympathy' that he felt was inevitable if he had to tell his mates in person. They wanted to find a way to take the edge off the initial communication and, after talking it through, they decided that the only way was to send a joint email telling their friends in a factual manner that they were separating and asking them to support them both. They were able to do that because their decision to separate was mutual and they had no ill will towards each other. They didn't want their friends to take sides, and that was where they found their strength.

They said that almost everyone had responded to their email saying thanks for letting them know and if they wanted help or support they were there for them. That is exactly what they had been looking for and so they felt confident that when they saw these friends, who were people they might bump into at the shops, or at someone's house, there wouldn't be that need to explain themselves over and over again. The email had precluded most of the questions. In it, they had asked friends to respect their wish to not fully disclose the reasons for their separation, saying that they both just felt the time had come and that it was best for both of them.

Although they had managed their friends fairly painlessly, Fiona and Rakesh felt less sure about their families. Rakesh said that although he was close to and got on well with Fiona's family, he was worried that they would blame him for the end of the marriage and their natural loyalty would be with her. He found thinking about what to say to them unbearable and his eyes would fill with tears.

So how could they best tell her large family, with whom they had a strong relationship? And his, which was much smaller, with most members living abroad and who didn't know much about their day-to-day lives?

Fiona agreed that Rakesh should call his family and tell them. She wanted him to communicate clearly that it was mutual and that she would be happy to be in touch with them if they ever wanted it. After much discussion, they agreed that they would both go and see

Fiona's family and, at a family meal, tell them all. Apart from Fiona's brother, nobody else had a clue. They knew that Fiona's other siblings, her parents, aunts and uncles would be shocked. They were both very nervous but fixed on a day to do it.

Rakesh and Fiona's story highlights some of the difficulties that arise when telling people. Finding a time and place that feel okay needs some thought. Often it is not possible to tell people together if one person has moved on before the other is ready or if there is little appetite for consensus or a benign separation. However, even if you can't communicate the separation together, sending an email to those you don't want to tell in person can be helpful, if you want to avoid answering lots of questions and endlessly repeating the same story.

If you choose to tell people yourself, you are entitled to say that you don't want to discuss the details. People don't have a right to know everything about your private life and you can tell them the 'headlines' without the minutiae. On the other hand, you may be someone who wants to tell it all, because it is a way of relieving the pain and it feels good to have a new audience. That is fine too.

There is no right or wrong way to tell your friends, family or work colleagues. You choose your method to suit you; you say only as much as you want to say and you stay in charge of what they know and what they don't know. People will take their cue from you. The more boundaries you set in the telling, the faster they will learn to listen and not ask too much. The more you tell and the more feeling you show, the more people are likely to know that you are not okay and try and stay in touch and continue to offer support. You can therefore determine what you need and what comes back to you.

Whichever way you choose to do it, you will get a variety of responses. For sure, some people will show concern and do their best to say and do the right thing. Others may seem misguided and unable to say anything right. Some may say tactless or provocative things that shock you. Ignore them; save your energies to make things better for yourself instead of wasting them on people who just don't get it. There are plenty of people who do, who will be there for you.

Telling friends and family is the beginning of the process. Once this is done, you are on your way to moving forwards and ultimately to leaving it all behind.

Saying nothing sometimes says the most.
Emily Dickinson

Managing conflict

Not all divorces and separations necessarily cause conflict. Sometimes a break-up can be amicable and collaborative, especially when it is as a result of a mutual feeling that there is no more mileage in the relationship. Even then, though, the process of separation can be a catalyst for all sorts of angry feelings that have previously been kept at bay. Now, with no need to keep the show on the road, diplomacy can be sacrificed on the altar of disappointment.

Conflict can also arise when the separation has been imposed on one person, particularly when there is tension around how much time is spent with children or there are disagreements about money.

In many divorce cases that I have seen, one partner has given assurances that the ex will not have to worry about money and then has not delivered on the promise. Similarly, assurances about contact with children for partners who have left are often unfulfilled, and they find themselves having to battle to see their children.

With or without children, there will come a time when finances and division of assets will eventually be resolved, if not by the two of you, then with the help of a mediator or through the court process. There will then be no need to continue a dialogue. You may still find it hard to achieve an emotional divorce but there will be nothing to fight about between you.

If you have children, conflict could potentially continue throughout their childhood, whilst you navigate and negotiate each change in circumstance as they grow.

The conflict will be, unwittingly, more about your individual internalised experiences of the world than what you are actually arguing about. Whilst you are ostensibly fighting over the details of, say, childcare arrangements, you can find yourself compelled to engage in a drawn-out battle about something with much deeper roots, a battle that you and your ex have probably rehearsed and aired many times before. It is a battle without end because unconsciously you are both invested in it.

How do you manage the conflict? It is understandably difficult when you are wounded and furious. I have many clients who say they just want peace but their ex is so provocative that they get drawn into something against their will. They ask, 'How can I create peace when my ex has a vested interest in making things difficult?' The fact is, it may well be your ex who is obstructive but you play your part in it too by engaging with it. If there is no take-up, he or she will have to move elsewhere to get a response. Bullies can only bully where there is fertile ground.

Ask yourself: how powerful is your ex in your mind? Why do you give them so much emotional space?

Perhaps you are drawn into a cycle despite your best intentions. Being drawn into a continual drama is another way of ensuring you remain in a relationship with your ex. It is painful but it staves off the feeling of being truly separated. The 'Letting go of grievance' and 'Feeling stuck' chapters might help you address these issues.

Watch what you do. Do you shoot off an email full of recriminations in response to your ex? Do you send a volley of texts because you have been wound up? Do you reel from a verbal attack and either withdraw from the world or lash out?

What to do

Turn your phone off at night and don't be tempted to look at it. If you need it on for other reasons, don't open anything that looks like it is from your ex. It can wait.

Don't respond to aggressive or provocative emails for 24 hours, unless they really warrant a response about an immediate arrangement. Then, sift through what is just provocation and *don't respond* to that bit at all. You don't need to give an answer to everything, and especially not the blaming bits. Don't grace provocation with a reaction. It is just too satisfying for your ex. If you do, you get drawn into a competitive feud in which no one feels they can afford to give any ground. It won't help you in the long run. You may be right, but at what price? Does your ex need to know you are right? No, only you need to know you are right.

Try, with all your communications, to take the sting

out of the message. Blame is a common currency but it never goes down well and just succeeds in achieving more polarisation rather than less. If you want a good response, then strategise. Think of the words you are going to use, carefully. The more measured you are, the more you are likely to get the reply you are looking for. If your considerable experience with your ex is that whatever you say or do you don't get a result, then stop. What is the point of going to a well that is dry?

You may think venting will get things off your chest. It won't make you feel better. Vent to your friends, or a counsellor or someone who will understand. There is no point airing grievances to someone who won't listen. You wouldn't usually bother to knock on a door that you know won't open. It is the same with your ex. If you know that you won't get the answer you are looking for, then don't ask, because the lack of answer will just be self-punishing.

If there are things that happen during contact that wind you up, please read the 'Common contact problems' chapter. Pick your battles. Manage conflict in that arena, too, by really thinking about what it is that you are reacting to. Ask yourself: are you creating or being part of a drama? Is it necessary? You could try disarming your ex by reacting in a way he or she doesn't expect. It can be very effective.

What is going on in conflict is the acting out of hurt and angry feelings. Rather than you both being able to say to each other what you feel, you start acting out those feelings, perhaps slamming the door in his face, or not coming to the door at all or taking up small slights like the fact that your child was delivered back 10 minutes late or was given something to eat that you don't approve of. Ask yourself: does that really matter? Or is it a way of communicating just how angry you are with the separation?

If you can stay on the side of your own life and work on how to enrich that rather than be drawn back again and again into something depleting for you, and which keeps you short of living it to the full, then that would be an achievement.

I facilitated a divorce support group of eight people. Nora was in her sixties and Sabine was in her thirties. Nora had divorced many years earlier but had never quite got over it. She thought a group would be helpful to her. Sabine was six months into her separation and had two young children. She was describing how angry she was with her ex and how she had not been able to stop herself shouting at him, in front of their children. She also said that she wouldn't let him have them for any overnight stays or let him speak to them when they were with her.

Nora told her that the one huge regret she had about her divorce was that it was long and painful and both she and her ex had fought bitterly, using the children as 'weapons'. What hurt her so much was that her children, now adults and a similar age to Sabine, told her frequently how they had missed out on their childhood and how they now hate conflict to the extent that they find any type of relationship difficult. She begged Sabine to learn from her situation, 'because it damages the children more than you can imagine'. Nora's story served as a powerful message to other members of the group who were younger than she was and didn't have the benefit of hindsight.

Managing conflict starts with you, and it will actually make you feel better. You can't control your ex's bad behaviour; you can only play your part. It is not a good feeling to be filled up with vengeance and animosity. It is better to think: I am not going to get what I need from my ex, so I will look elsewhere, firstly to myself and then to others who will appreciate me and be happy to make me feel good about myself. Once your ex picks up that you are no longer interested in the tortuous dance, he or she may just have to do something different.

How we choose our partners

So many clients have asked me why they have ended up with the sort of partner they have and talk about their fear that, once divorced, they will attract the same sort of person again. They are worried that they are doomed to replicate their past experience and never be free to love and be loved in a more satisfying way.

How do we choose our partners? On the face of it, we choose people who we are attracted to physically and mentally. We like our partners to make us laugh, make us feel loved, and be people who we can respect and think of as clever and reliable. But so much else goes on that we are not even aware of when we start to fall in love.

Sometimes people just turn out to be disappointing, not what they seemed; but more often what happens is that, when things go wrong, we look back and say they were always a bit like that, we just chose to ignore it. When we meet someone, we are picking up signals from him or her and unconsciously calibrating them. The more we pick up signals that are familiar, the more we fall in love. That is fine if what is familiar was a good enough experience, but what if it wasn't?

If your early experiences were less than satisfactory,

for example a neglectful mother or a violent father, you will want to avoid that when choosing a relationship; however, often we end up with someone who is very similar to that dysfunctional parent without realising it.

Roxie said, 'At the beginning, I thought he was so nice and so different from my father who had affairs throughout my childhood. I see now that he was exactly the same, but how could I have known that?'

By understanding our early relationships with our parents, we are better placed to avoid endlessly re-enacting experiences that will usually get us nowhere. We often unwittingly 'marry the parent' that we had the most dysfunctional relationship with in an unconscious bid to 'fix' it. If our unconscious has done its powerful job, we will find that we can't fix it, but are destined to replicate similar painful early experiences within the relationship. Often our partner will be the other side of the equation – not only are they a repeat for us of what we had, but we are a repeat for him or her of their early lives.

In other words, there is a fitting of experience unconsciously set up to suit both people. *A perfect, imperfect match.* Only it's a painful way of having a relationship and often ends in trouble.

Georgie was fed up with being in a relationship with a man who blew hot and cold. She didn't know on a daily basis where she was with him. Sometimes he was critical and cruel, then full of remorse and eager to get back in with her. Although the abusive nature of his actions was intolerable, the loving side always drew her back in. She couldn't understand why she had put up with it for so long but at the same time argued that she couldn't leave because she was so worried about what would happen to him if she left him on his own.

I talked with Georgie about when her husband was being nice and kind: the 'evidence' of the abuse was somehow wiped out of her mind and she wasn't able to think. Georgie told me that she was brought up with an alcoholic father. He would rage and then calm down and be very remorseful. When he wasn't drinking he was often depressed and Georgie used to worry about him and do everything she could to bring him out of it. It never worked and she found herself in a state of constant worry about what would happen to her father and, by extension, to her.

Georgie had found a way of unconsciously replicating her childhood experience in her adult relationships. Although her partner wasn't an alcoholic, his moods were changeable and erratic and she was forever trying to reconcile with him and then panicking when he was in a state.

By understanding what had inadvertently driven her to hook up with her partner, Georgie was better equipped to do something different in the future and give herself a chance to be in a meaningful non-abusing relationship.

We need not only to understand why we are unconsciously drawn to certain people but also to develop sufficiently to dispense with that 'fix' and avoid recreating the familiar experience. Sometimes the insight isn't enough; we need to *grow* sufficiently to not need the 'fix' of the bad experience

Once we have achieved that, we are open to new possibilities and people who will enable us to flourish.

If your experience of life with your partner resonates with these descriptions, then your separation will be a spring board from which you can have future relationships which aren't a repetition of something unhealthy. Your separation will have given you an opportunity to have a better and more meaningful experience.

No matter how hard the world pushes against me, within me, there's something stronger – something better, pushing right back.

Albert Camus

Coping with a new partner in your ex's life

It is often at this stage that things can feel intolerable. Whilst you might have been able to deal with the separation, there is something about a third person entering the arena that seems to change everything.

All sorts of uncomfortable feelings might emerge now, including the worry that your children are going to be involved with another family and may be seduced into wanting to spend more time in the other home. Maybe there are step-siblings for your children or even a new baby. Things seem more comfortable and easy for your ex than for you. You are struggling and feeling left out and forgotten. It feels like he or she has got it all and you are just left with all the feelings.

'He/she has got away scot free'

In my experience, having to deal with a new partner in an ex's life can be both a significant milestone on the road to separation and a serious flashpoint. Much of what you are feeling now seems a bit nightmarish – out of all proportion, even waking you at 3am… only in this case the dawn doesn't seem to come. You may be imagining that your ex is having a wonderful life full of family and friends and everything that you crave. You construct an idyll in your mind which makes you feel bleaker than ever before.

Well, let me tell you that this wonderful new life is a myth. It is not real. Your ex will have his or her own worries and feelings about the separation and difficulties with everyday life just like everyone else. Only it is hard for you to see that right now (and your ex certainly won't admit to such worries or put them on display).

You may be feeling very low, very small and marginalised. You may feel on the outside of everything: of the new couple, of the new family, of former friendships. Contrary to what your internal world is telling you, it is *your* life that is important. You *are* the centre of that and in charge of that. Take a step back to look at *your* life, and try and go some way to making it what you want it to be. You are not helpless, or hopeless, or unable to have an impact. You are a whole person, with thoughts, opinions, beliefs, desires, passions and interests.

People leaving and turning their backs on us taps into the earliest feelings of loss and abandonment that we experience in childhood when we are dependent on other people. You are an adult, though; you are not that powerless child who is doing his or her best to drag you backwards to a helpless state.

You need to recognise that it is those parts of yourself that you have buried – those powerful early emotions – that are being triggered and contributing to you feeling so angry and helpless.

What to do

Every time you think of your ex with his or her new partner, visualise the word STOP, or imagine a red traffic light. Stop, and go back to thinking of your own life and how you can make it better. Do this every time. It will get easier and become a habit.

Remember that the idea that your ex and his or her partner are having a wonderful life is a story that you are telling yourself and it is one that constantly wounds you. It is a type of self-harm story, but it is not one you are reading, it is one you are *writing*. You are its author. Be aware of that and try to use different words to describe it. What's more, the new partner is often jealous of your ex's marriage with you, the pull of the children from that marriage, the pull of family events, and it creates tension. So when you feel left out, think about that.

Joelle and Simon were experiencing problems in their relationship. They had got together when Simon had been unhappy in his marriage. They had been together for two years and their new baby was 10 months old. Joelle was very frustrated and upset because Simon went to see his three boys from his marriage on alternate weekends. Their mother wanted him to come to the family home to pick them up and take them out to spend time just with them because they missed him. Joelle said that she should be as important as his children. She understood he needed to see them but she wanted him to see them less often and bring them to their new home rather than spend the day out with them. She felt he was prioritising them over his new family. Simon felt torn. He desperately wanted to maintain a meaningful relationship with his three children and understood that they needed some undivided attention. He also wanted to go back to the family home for their birthday events and go to school parents' evenings to show them that he hadn't abandoned them. He wanted Joelle to understand and support him in that. Joelle felt she couldn't unless he showed his other family how important *she* was. Simon was telling her that she was important but that, having taken on someone with responsibilities already in place, she couldn't simply delete that family in her mind and be 'the only one'.

Life in a new relationship is rarely as easy as it may look. Simon's ex-wife may well have thought that he had moved on and not looked back, but that was not the case.

In fact, there is often tension in new relationships because the new partner is jealous of the attention that their partner pays to his or her first family.

You will understandably have little or no sympathy for the woman or man that your ex is now with, but it is important to know that life is definitely not all rosy on the other side of the equation. You should remember this when you are feeling that your life is less than. In fact, your life is more than, as you can make it whatever you want it to be.

So, when you feel like this outside person, it is important to *reflect* on what is happening. The case study above will show you that the reality is different from the story you are writing in your mind.

Separation triggers so many early *un*-thought about experiences and sometimes we are at the mercy of them when they are stirred up by life events. We start to occupy the position of the abandoned child, and feel left out. It is a state of mind. Try to do one thing each day for yourself, not just as a distraction but as a way of making your life significant to you. Go to the gym or for a walk, meet a friend, book a concert, or arrange a lunch. Instead of feeling on the outside of someone else's life, create a way of being that puts you on the inside of yours. To help you start to 'own' your own life, do the Self-esteem exercise at the back of this book.

Ways of managing

I asked my group members to write down one thing that was helping them during this very difficult time. This is what they said:

Making new friends
Gardening
Staying off alcohol
Seeing someone
Talking to someone
Change of location
Keeping a journal
Taking small steps
Self-help books
Sleep
Music
Support groups
Eating healthily
Listening to the radio
Running
Praying
Swimming
Seeing relatives
Keeping a routine

Small treats
Making plans for the future
Walking
Yoga
Playing with their children
Taking one day at a time
The feeling of winning
Home-making
Counselling

Recalibrating your expectations

We all know that if we expect something and it doesn't happen we feel disappointed. Once we have a bank of experience from our shared life with someone to draw on, we know what to expect and what not to expect from them. If we know that, despite all our longing and hopes, something is not going to be, then surely we are foolish to keep on hoping? Some may say it is positively masochistic. We manage to somehow 'trick' ourselves to keep on longing for something that just won't happen. Much as we may want to, we can't simply turn hope off like a tap.

If you are feeling really fed up and exhausted with this state of mind, it is time to recalibrate your expectations. In broad terms, you need to realign them and signpost them in the direction of reality, towards something that will begin to meet your needs and your hopes.

For example, you may be hoping that your partner will see sense and come back. How often have I heard people say, 'He doesn't know what his doing, he is having a mid-life crisis, I think he is having some sort of break-down.' You may cling to the idea that his or her new partner will come to seem inadequate and a mistake. If a friend said this to you about her own break-up, you would very likely be saying (or at least thinking): that is not right and that won't happen. Why is it so easy to give advice but not adhere to any that you would give someone else? Why is it that the wise words you happily offer to a friend just don't apply to you? It is not easy to override the compulsion to believe that your ex will come back, but the alternative is to live with feeling constantly let down, upset and powerless. If, however, you can loosen the grip that your ex has on you, you will be free to live your own life again.

The circular thinking and expecting that gets you nowhere becomes a bit addictive. It's as though you are programmed to keep going back for something you won't get. Being aware of it is the first step. Do a double-take every single time you do it. It will then become less easy to fall prey to it. Think to yourself: is he or she really going to change? Is he or she going to do the thing I ask? If, based on history, the answer is likely to be 'no', then turn your thoughts elsewhere. Do something different. Change the record and you will start to enjoy the new record. It is so liberating to stop being caught up in something that is harmful for you on a daily basis.

Significant calendar days of the year

When you have broken up with someone, all sorts of things, like places and dates, seem more meaningful than they might have before. They can highlight feelings of loneliness, isolation or that you are somehow just unacknowledged.

The days that tend to resonate are birthdays, Christmas, New Year's Eve, Mother's or Father's Day. Unfortunately, the calendar year is peppered with 'significant' days that are to be marked or remembered, and it is the memories of how you spent them when you were with your partner that might fill your mind rather than thoughts of how to manage the day now so that it feels good for you. However, these are just days, and they will pass.

One client said that she never used to take much notice of Mother's Day but after her partner left, it made her feel very alone, perhaps because she became more conscious of the fact that it was she who was left looking after the children's day-to-day needs. She managed it by hooking up with friends with children of the same age and having a big celebratory lunch.

Christmas, Chanukah and Eid are days that may have enormous significance even if you are not religious, as the emphasis is on family and friends and being together. If you have children, it is particularly painful not to be with them, and to think of them perhaps having a good time with your ex and his or her new partner.

If you find yourself endlessly thinking about your ex being free as a bird to do what he or she wants, you are only harming yourself. Ask yourself why you are choosing to do this and place yourself in the role of victim rather than make things good for yourself. As with all the events that trigger more extreme feelings of being on the outside, the trick is to picture yourself involved and included in something that *you* belong to and are a part of. If you haven't got an invitation or there isn't something obvious happening that you can join in on, try to create something. Do something different rather than clinging to the familiar patterns and routines. The more you engage with life, the more it will engage you. The only thing holding you back is you.

Can you try and allow yourself to triumph by being the capable, competent person that you are?

In the depth of winter, I finally learned that within me there lay an invincible summer.

Albert Camus

Separating when you are over 50

In the last decade, more people than ever before, in their fifties, sixties and seventies, have separated and are continuing to do so. A whole generation is embracing the idea that we are living longer and so have the time to have a second chance to get it right. Our philosophy of life in the 21st century is kinder and less puritanical than that of previous centuries; it says that we are entitled to find happiness and that we don't have to endure the unendurable. For many now reaching late-middle age, the idea of a second chance can offer a new lease of life but it can also feel frightening.

Often older people feel that they have worked at their marriages all their lives with a view to retiring together and putting into place plans that may have been deferred for years. They may have waited for children to leave home and establish themselves before starting to live out their dreams as a couple. If at this stage you are left, it can feel very much like the rug has been pulled from beneath you and the plans you had been harbouring for so many years have crumbled into dust. As one person put it, 'All I have worked towards has gone.' That would be true only if you had no faith in your ability to function without a partner. When you are used to being a couple for a long time, it is easy to think you can't stand on your own two feet. You will have to do just a few of the exercises in this book to realise that that isn't true. In fact, the longer you have lived, the more you will be able to draw on a long list of competencies. You have probably been the CEO of your relationship, your family, your life.

If your long marriage is over, you have the chance to get things right for yourself. If it is your partner who has left, you may have a sneaking suspicion that, although it wasn't your decision and you wouldn't have made it, life hasn't actually been all that rosy for you. You may have endured a lot and, however old you are, there is an opportunity now to do something different, to convert safety and predictability into something creative and new.

You need to have courage to do that. We only have one life; you need to make it the best it can be. What is the alternative? Is it to mourn forever, to let the possibility of new experiences pass you by? You have the choice to accept the circumstances and see what can be built out of them. To use age as a way of restricting that ability to grab life is to use it as an excuse rather than as a reality. The unknown is always frightening but as you start to see all the opportunities available to you, your fear will diminish.

Take your time to mourn, to grieve, to be angry and then go right out there and embrace your new life. You have already had a life well lived on one road, so you know you are good at it. Now it's time to take another. You can still travel, if that was the plan; you just need to find other people to do it with, if you don't want to go alone.

Age brings wisdom, experience and respect from others. Harness it to your advantage. Use what you have learned over many years to feed you rather than deplete you. You can still do all the things that you have dreamed of.

Ruby was in her late sixties. She was full of a fiery determination that, having separated from her husband, she would not go back to him. She described a long marriage, during which she felt she had had little joy, and yet they had stuck together through thick and thin. She had been lonely in her relationship and was often envious of what she thought other couples appeared to have. She wanted to leave before it was too late.

However, she felt guilty, leaving him on his own after all these years. She also felt scared that her feisty resolve would disappear if it proved difficult to start again. Her dilemma was: should she take what looked like the safer path, staying loyal to the marriage, her family and friends, or break for the border and take a risk in the hope of finding happiness?

She discovered through talking that, for her, staying in her unhappy marriage had been debilitating and had sapped her energy and enthusiasm for life. We talked a lot about what she was looking for and how she saw herself living in the future. She knew that it was very different from starting anew in her thirties or forties; she was unable to work, she didn't have the same energy to go out all the time and she questioned whether it was better to live with someone grumpy and not particularly caring than to live on her own. However, although it was comforting to live with the familiar, she knew that what she needed was a fresh start. She said her friends would be shocked but she couldn't stay to meet their expectations.

As the weeks went by, Ruby began to live in a way that seemed totally new to her. On a micro level, she rejoiced in the fact that she no longer had to put food on the table for her husband or be mindful of what he needed and wanted. She realised that there were lots of people in a similar situation who were also longing to start living again. On a wider level, the more she saw how much she had been missing out on, the more enthusiastic she became about living every moment to the full. There was mourning to be done for what she felt she had lost, and for the things she'd never had in her marriage, but she was relieved not to have to face a daily reminder of how there was nothing left between them.

Ruby is a good example of how you can turn things around. Whether you have no choice because you have been left or you have taken the courageous decision to leave yourself, life is never static. Ruby went with it rather than let it pass her by.

Giving history a rewrite

You probably have a collection of photos that tell the story of your relationship and your family. Holidays, birthdays or anniversaries, pictures of the two of you raising a glass to the camera. They may be difficult to look at now, evoking memories that would have been sweet before separation but are now bitter or painful.

The photos are just one part of the 'evidence' of your relationship which now takes on a different meaning; and, having broken up, you may find yourself re-evaluating your relationship and turning it in your mind from a success into a sham.

There is definitely another way of looking at this. You have rewritten your relationship in the light of its unwanted outcome. It does you a great disservice. A long-term relationship isn't a failure just because it ended. You don't need to strip it of its worth. A relationship that lasts longer is no more or less successful than a shorter one or one that comes to an end painfully.

The memories which come to mind when you look at your photos are of the things you did together and the life you created then. It may be hard to look at them now but they are evidence of something good that was sustained for the period that it lasted. Divorce or separation shouldn't negate what you had. Spending however many years with a person in a meaningful way is anything but a failure. If you have children together, they are the tangible product of the success of your relationship.

The fact that you have had even one significant relationship tells you that you are more than capable of going on to have another, because you have the capacity to relate. That is no mean achievement.

We navigate by stories, but sometimes we only escape by abandoning them.

Rebecca Solnit

Creating a different story

When you talk to friends and family about your break-up, does it seem to you that you sound a bit like a looped tape, repeating your painful narrative over and over?

You may notice that the more you tell your story, the more fixed it becomes. This is significant because the story itself becomes not only how people see you but, more importantly, how you see yourself. It can define, and then restrict you. It can make a significant contribution to your feeling of being stuck (see the 'Feeling stuck' chapter).

If good friends are listening closely to you and see you within the prescriptive frame of how you describe yourself, they will unwittingly collude with you and your story. You will have given them no language to help you out. They will be left with little choice but to repeat it back to you with sympathy, or tell you to move on. They won't be able to help you think about it in a different and open way.

We limit ourselves by the stories we tell and, in the telling of them; we forget that we can expand the meaning or colour of that story, just by using different words to describe it. If you can do that, it will provide the possibility of a way out, of seeing things from a different perspective. In other words, you can reframe it.

What, then, might it be like to tell the same story but from a different angle?

Story 1, set in stone = stuck

My husband left me and the children and I am so angry. It is really difficult for me and the children and I don't want to have anything to do with him. My life is depressing and rather limited now. I don't know how he could do this to me. Everything is a struggle.

Story 2, flexible = free

My husband left me and I feel tremendously sad, frightened and angry. I wish he hadn't done this; it has really made things difficult for me and the children, but it has also given me an opportunity to show that I am strong and creative. I know that life is full of curve balls and I am going to try and convert this one into something that works. I won't always feel like this. There is more to me than this separation.

The facts are the same in both versions; her husband has left her and she has all sorts of understandable feelings about it. But, the *stories* are different. The second story moves her forward: from being a victim of circumstance to being a creative, courageous person who has some power to determine her own destiny.

The question to ask is: *Is this story I keep repeating helping me?* The answer more likely than not, is no.

Your separation does not define you. It is a real and significant part of your story, but it is *never* the whole story. The whole story of you is much more complicated and involves many other thoughts, feelings and experiences which need to be kept alive rather than drowned by the noise of your separation.

It is easy, if painful, to think of yourself as just the victim of someone else's behaviour. It seems much harder to tell a story about you sticking up for yourself.

Being a victim does put you in a powerful position, because it means all the aggression is located in your ex. However, it doesn't help you, because as a victim you are unable to use your own potency and live your life properly. Giving up that dance may feel like the hardest thing. However, it can also be very empowering, because it forces you to recognise that you too played some role, even if only a small one, in the breakdown of your relationship. You were not just a passive recipient in it.

In life, when bad things happen we can feel like the object of misfortune and nothing else. In fact, we are always *both and*, not *either or*: *both* the victim *and* the person who *does*.

The story of two positions, either victim or villain (and more often than not you describe yourself as the former) gets in the way of an emotional resolution.

Once you start to see this rounder picture of yourself, you will begin to move towards a more complex, realistic narrative of your life. If you can gradually do this, you will also be inspiring others with your story of courage, survival, creativity and hope.

We are not what happened to us, we are what we wish to become.

Carl Jung

Thinking about the positives

Remember: it is your divorce and you will move through the stages only when you are ready to. Now may not be the right time for you to think about any positives associated with separation. If this is so, come back to this chapter later. If you do feel ready, take some time to think about what the positives might be. Here is a list of feelings that people in my support groups have shared as the positives of separation:

Opportunity
Hope for the future
Excitement
Re-addressing
Developing
Adventure
Liberating
New possibilities
Optimism
Energy
Feeling whole
Reclaiming yourself
Confidence
Being present

Freedom
Self-reliance
Space for others
Self-esteem
Focused

Once you have moved through all the stages of divorce or separation and the feelings linked to it, you will get to the point where you realise that being a single adult can be an exciting, interesting, worthwhile and meaningful way of living. How creative it is, to be in charge of your own life, to be free, to choose your own way of doing things, your own interests and your own friends. It is not about being alone; it is about choosing people who don't restrict you, who share your new ideas about the world.

It is about breaking out of your own personal prison which the separation and its mourning process have kept you in. You will begin to feel that the prison door has opened and that nothing is keeping you in it but yourself. Start to walk towards the door and then walk right through it. You will have left the prison of self-pity, recrimination and grievance and be free to embrace your new life as your own person.

Sharing your children

One of the things that is really distressing when you separate is the need to share your children. You may feel fiercely possessive of them, whilst recognising that they do need a relationship with both parents. The idea of your children living and moving between two households is one that is hard to come to terms with. All the time they are with your ex they are not with you. Whether or not you despise your ex, not spending all your leisure time with your kids feels very painful and sometimes lonely. It can also feel like an affront to your idea of bringing up a family – that you can cope with everything else being split between you but not the children.

To be without your children when they bring life and distraction into your household just puts you more in touch with your grief. Negotiating contact or contact itself can become the most fertile territory for upset and animosity between you and your ex – an opportunity for you to make him or her feel the full force of your fury and hurt.

Some people manage their children being away by seeing it as a time to catch up with friends, pursue interests or just relax after a busy working week; an opportunity rather than a loss. They are confident in the knowledge that their children will come back with all their mess and noise. At a time when you need to regroup and rethink the map of your life, this can provide you with an ideal window.

Unfortunately, knowing that it is good for your children to have an ongoing relationship with both of you does not stop it hurting. There is likely to be a conflict between what you feel is right for them and what you feel is right for you.

Barbara, who came to the group, said, 'If I let him have them for the weekend of his birthday, he will have got everything he wants. He is getting on with his life without a thought for me.' She was so wounded by the break-up that holding onto the children seemed like the only way she could feel like she had something that he didn't. She said that if she said 'no' it would be so upsetting for him that it would give him an experience of what she was feeling. It made her feel better.

It can be difficult to witness your ex enjoying a relationship with your children, when you feel that what he or she has done to you and subsequently the family is tantamount to a crime. Some people say 'He has left us' rather than 'He has left me' and the children then become pawns in the fight between the two of you. When taken to extremes, this behaviour becomes what is known as parental alienation: one parent recruits the children to his or her view of the ex to such an extent that it severs the bond between them.

For you it may be less extreme than that, but

occasionally you might notice yourself subtly attempting to drop little ideas into your children's minds to try and make them see your ex from your point of view. It can seem hard to resist doing so, especially when you are so distressed.

Another parent, Phoebe, said that as her ex had gone off with someone else, he had obviously left the family, not just her, and that she had told the children so in no uncertain terms. The children, taking their cue from their mother, started to hate the dad they used to love, or at least that is what they said. No matter how many entreaties he made towards them, showing that he still wanted to see them and be with them, they only saw him in the light of what he had done to the family and didn't believe him.

Phoebe said, 'I am not objecting to them spending time with him; they can see him if they want to, they just don't want to because they can see for themselves what he has done to us.' Phoebe had done an effective job of alienating the children and had then convinced herself that she hadn't by saying that she didn't stop them seeing their dad. She firmly believed that they were free to say they wanted to see him and that they truly didn't want to. And they, in their turn, just couldn't afford to break rank and did a good job of convincing themselves and their mother that they were no longer interested in their dad.

What had really happened was that the children had ended up feeling guilty about wanting a relationship with their dad and guilty about missing him. It is very difficult for a child in those circumstances to negotiate their own relationship because they can't talk to their parents honestly about it.

This is deeply damaging for children, as they know they are made up of both parents, and so to witness one parent being denigrated makes them feel that there must be something intrinsically 'wrong' with *them*. When children are drawn into conflict and used as judges of their other parent, they are not free to be themselves. They feel they have to hide how much they enjoy contact or what they have done during the weekend with their dad or their mum. They begin to live in a split world, where they can't talk to either parent about their experience with the other for fear of contributing to upset. They start to pretend that things aren't that good or they start to keep secrets, staying quiet rather than talking.

George was 43. He had been married for 15 years and he had left his wife. He was desperate to have an easier relationship with his four children. His ex had told the children that 'Daddy has left us' and he felt devastated. He told me, weeping, that he had not left his children. He loved them and he was really worried that they would start to buy into their mother's version of events. He knew that she was angry with him and justifiably so, but he felt that she punished him through the children. All arrangements to see the children had to go through their mother and he had no say. If he brought them back three minutes late, she would be standing on the doorstep ready to shout at him. If he was early the same happened. She would leave notes in their overnight bags telling him what he should feed them and what time they should go to bed. He would inevitably get a call from her in the middle of the week to let him know that the children had told her something about the contact weekend that had made her angry and he then found that she would cancel the next contact under some pretext of an unavoidable event. He got letters from her lawyer telling him that the children were not to be left on a Saturday night with his parents (their grandparents) whilst he went out for a couple of hours and that if he did that, she wouldn't allow him to see them. He felt that every aspect of his relationship with his children was proscribed by his ex and he felt powerless.

It wasn't just George getting hurt; the children were picking up on it and were worried about both their parents. They worked out really quickly that they were important in the war between their parents, and didn't know what to say to each of them to keep them happy.

You really don't want your children to be weapons of hurt. You want them to be children free to love and be loved. In terms of their own relationships as adults, being in the middle of a battle doesn't help them in any shape or form.

Paul, in our group, said that his wife wanted him to see the children more than once a week and for them to stay over. She told him that she needed a break and the children really missed him. He told the group that he wasn't going to let her boss him around and that he would see them when he wanted and not when she said. He wasn't going to see them so that she could have a break to see her boyfriend. He wasn't a babysitter. The group helped him see that the only people who really suffered from his anger towards his ex-wife were his three small children. They were, in fact, desperate to see him but in his bid to score points he had lost sight of that. The next week he came back and told the group that he had set up overnight stays and the children were delighted. He could see that his legitimate anger towards his ex-wife was having an impact on his children, who were not to blame for anything that had gone on between their parents.

I have heard many a parent say that Saturday to Sunday on alternate weekends with their other parent is enough for the children; that otherwise they need to be at home. On further exploration, it becomes clear that it isn't the children who need to be at home but the parent who needs them there because their absence intensifies the loneliness. These are very understandable feelings. The task is to manage them and find a place to talk about them without using the children to relieve them.

Often mothers talk about how their children's father took very little interest in the children until they separated and then suddenly he became a 'divorce-activated dad'. This becomes another reason why the children shouldn't see much of him: he doesn't deserve it.

'The children adore him; they can't see what he is really like.'

Women often feel that, even though they work, they

do most of the childcare, so why should they have to give the children up at weekends and not enjoy more leisure time with them? Whereas men worry that if they are not living with their children, they will lose their link with them. They feel that as children live mostly with their mother, they miss out on the day-to-day.

Some women also feel ambivalent about the role of the father, on the one hand wanting him to be involved on some level and on the other believing he is not good enough.

All these things are more to do with your feelings towards your ex and about the separation than with what is necessarily right for the children. We all have our children's best interests at heart but how those best interests are interpreted depends very much on whether you can see that *their* relationship with your ex is separate from *your* feelings about your ex.

What can be helpful here is for both parties to be mindful that they need to show some respect for each other's feelings – whether they are the one who is hurt at having been left, or the one who feels guilty about what they have done; and contact arrangements should be conducted in an amicable way, however hard it is.

Jay and Fran were trying to work out the children's contact schedule. He had moved out and was living with his new partner. She was scathing towards him and her distress was entirely understandable. The children were young and she couldn't believe that he had walked out on her for someone else. What made it worse was that, when she was trying to draw up a schedule, he would say, 'Carine needs me that weekend so I can't do that' or 'Carine doesn't want me coming to the family home more than once a month.' The mere mention of Carine's name and the idea that his contact with his children was determined by what his new partner wanted made any attempt at arrangements impossible.

I wondered whether it was possible for them to talk to each other about contact as a parental couple without bringing a third party into the negotiations. If Jay felt compromised by his new partner, I wondered if he could simply say that he wasn't available at a particular time, without rubbing salt in the wound by saying it was his new girlfriend who was effectively calling the shots. The impact of his insensitivity to Fran meant that she could no longer be rational about the children and retreated to a place that felt safer and where she couldn't be hurt by him. As a consequence, she made it almost impossible for him to see the children unless he came to the house and saw them there. It was her way of getting back at him and her way of showing his girlfriend who was in charge.

How to avoid this

The question to bear in mind when you are deciding about contact is this:

Is denying contact, or being difficult about it, a kicking you want to give your ex or is your decision truly just for the benefit of the children? Is what you are arranging with your ex more about revenge, or more about your children's needs?

If you can keep that in mind, it may make the sharing of your children a little bit easier – not just for them but also for you. It is exhausting to be constantly in battle mode and it doesn't make you happier.

It might help to think of your children as independent separate beings who are entitled to have relationships with both parents, if those relationships are available. That way they will be relieved of the burden of feeling that they have to look after the parent who is trying to hold onto them.

Managing your children's experience of divorce

What are your children to make of your divorce? What impact will it have on them? One of your concerns, if not your main concern, will be how they will manage.

Try to hold in mind that their experience of separation is entirely different from yours. No one is severing a relationship with them. They are not getting divorced. And their primary relationships with both parents will remain intact and continue throughout their childhood.

Your separation will be unsettling and upsetting for them but there is no need for it to be devastating if you handle it right. One of the things that makes it manageable for children is the idea that both of you feel that you are vital to them.

Parents often worry that their children feel exactly the same way they do. This usually isn't the case. Children are only concerned about whether you are okay and will survive and what their lives moving forward will look like. If you can reassure them about both those things you will be going a long way to making things good for them.

This is why it is essential to keep any hostility between

the two of you away from your children. Otherwise, they will grow up needing to keep everything separate, for example not mentioning Mum to Dad in Dad's house and vice versa. If they do this, they will live in a split universe, which is unhealthy. They need to see how *you* manage conflict and how you negotiate things on their behalf. They can then grow into adults able to integrate experiences and able to manage potential difficulties with ease.

Children are often hyper-vigilant, especially when they feel a little unsafe. They will scrutinise your facial expressions, silently picking up on conversations which you believe are out of earshot, and trying to make sense of it all. Of course, there is no avoiding that you may have overwhelming feelings and feel very angry or upset. It is important not to pretend that everything is fine when they will see it clearly isn't. But you can say, 'I do feel upset but it will all be okay and with time I will feel better.' That is a far cry from 'Your dad has really been nasty to me and I don't want him coming to the front door to pick you up.' The latter puts your children in a conflicted position, feeling bad for you and also feeling worried for themselves as clearly their dad will be coming to pick them up.

A dose of reality is important, so long as it is understood that this is *your* experience and you are not inviting your children to get involved with it.

Your children will also need some help in managing their feelings. The idea is not to take their feelings away but to give them some coping mechanisms. You may have a child who doesn't freely share what she is thinking and you may be wondering what to do to help her talk. It may be that, in her eyes, the parent who has left has fallen from grace and she may be furious. She may be angry with both of you for not staying together. When she finds out about a possible third party, if it is very near the beginning of the separation, she may feel very stirred up and an idolised parent may be temporarily demoted. Of course, all these are understandable feelings and she will need your help to cope with them.

Communication is the key, even if it seems to be you doing all the communicating. A silent child is not a child who is not listening. Also, she must not pick up the idea that to tell you how she feels will upset you, or she will never speak.

Children may long to reunite their family. But actually the more they see that the separation is permanent and managed, the quicker they too can be okay with it.

Your child may be good at 'acting out' his feelings and not very good at articulating them. We adults are often the same. For example, your child may come home shouting, being stroppy and out of sorts. Sometimes a description of what is happening can be helpful. 'I see you are very cross about something right now, perhaps you can tell me what it is when you have stopped shouting.' Then, when he is calm later, you can say, 'I noticed how cross you seemed; I wonder if you can say what it was that was making you feel so bad.'

Just as with you, naming feelings to help him understand them is a way to make him feel more connected with you so that he can then think, 'Mum and Dad understand.' Try to avoid shouting at your child when he is behaving badly during this difficult period: you don't want to push him even further into his confused state.

What he needs is for you to help him think and process and give back his often unwanted feelings in a more manageable, modified form. So instead of getting cross, stop and think about what might be happening; show him you notice the feeling, not the behaviour, and then try to contain the behaviour. Afterwards, when he feels understood, he may be able to express in words how he feels rather than through his behaviour.

Children need to know, and for it to be shown in practice, that there is no judgement attached to them seeing their other parent; they need to know that the practical arrangements will be kept to and to know the boundaries and structure of them.

If your children are teenagers, they will be acting out royally over all sorts of things. You may, because you feel guilty, automatically attribute any bad behaviour to your separation. But of course children in families where the parents are together *also* behave badly at times, especially as teenagers. It is part of the process of breaking away and becoming independent. Kicking against you is part of their development. It is the only way they know of creating sufficient distance to make them believe they can manage developing into an independent adult. So give yourself a break and don't make it your default mode to think it is all the fault of the divorce.

Common contact problems

The following is a list of what some of you may find frustrating when your children spend time with their other parent:

- Watching too much TV
- Not doing their homework
- Being given too many presents
- Clothes not being brought back
- Clothes coming back dirty
- Being allowed to stay up too late
- Being fed pizzas and unhealthy things
- Not being brought back on time

You may have found that differences emerge between you in the way you look after your children; perhaps they are differences that were there before that have simply come into sharp focus on separation. What seemed good enough the day before you separated seems to be intolerable the day after. You may not have noticed the way that your ex looked after your children when you were living together, or maybe at the time it didn't feel like an insurmountable problem. Now it seems to trigger an allergic reaction in you.

It may be that your ex is riddled with guilt and wants to overcompensate by being indulgent. It may be that routines in the other household are just at odds with the structures you have put into place in your home. It is understandably annoying and creates anxiety in you.

If you step back, though, and look at those differences in a wider context, they may feel less acute. Compare them to neglect or maltreatment, and they lose some of their significance. Is the situation really that bad or is it more that anything your ex does, especially with your children who you miss, will feel wrong?

Rachel, in one of our groups, felt bereft when the children were away for the weekend and it hurt that they seemed to have a good time. She was completely conflicted. She didn't want them to have a bad time, but it was galling to hear how they had enjoyed their time with her ex. Rather than working through that, she came up with reasons to 'spoil' the idea of the children's good experience by finding fault with bed times, lack of routine, her ex getting together with their mutual friends, and so on.

Take a good look at what is going on, and decide what is really a problem and what is a distraction in order to release yourself from being tied into what is restricting and limiting for you. Recognising that it is something to do with your understandable feelings about loss rather than about contact will help you reclaim your life. Your children will come back after visits and they will still love you. You can be as sure of that as you can be of anything. That is what is important.

What is really going on with contact problems

People often complain that their attempts to make contact with their children when they are with the other parent are met with avoidance. You might have given them a mobile phone so that they can be in touch, only to find that it is constantly switched off, or the children are 'not allowed' to use it. Sometimes a dad might ask, as the children will be staying just round the corner at their mum's house during the holidays, whether he could see them for just an hour so that it isn't so long until he sees them again. The answer is often no.

This is not about what is good for the children but more about scoring points and giving the other parent an experience of the hurt you are feeling. You know the impact on your ex of not allowing him or her to phone but you do it precisely because it will hurt. You may believe that it doesn't have an impact on the children, but it does: they know that phoning their mum during contact with dad will upset their dad and not phoning will upset their mum.

Similarly, they know that if they choose not to return with a new present they have been given, it will upset the parent who gave it to them. In this way, children become possessions that you each want to keep to yourself rather than people who can love both their parents freely, regardless of whether they are with one or the other.

Your children should be learning how conflict gets

resolved, how arrangements are managed and how people collaborate with each other. If you and your ex use shared contact as a way of hurting each other, the only people who really get hurt are the children. They will be taking it all in. They will be asking themselves what they have done to make their parents so cross and they will be developing false selves to accommodate the moods and feelings of both their parents so as not to contribute to their sadness.

How children behave around contact

It is very common for children, particularly very young ones, to not want to go for contact and, if they go, to come back having tantrums and behaving really badly. It is just as hard for them as it is for you to nego-tiate their re-entry into the way of your household after contact.

Often children don't want to go because they are anxious and worried about you. Will you manage without them, will you survive, will you be too unhappy? They are going to see the person who they know has caused you hurt or who they know you don't have warm feelings towards. They will feel guilty and conflicted. If you are their primary carer they will not want to do anything that will harm you so theywill say what you might like to hear.

What to do

You will need to show your children when they come home that you are fine. Tell them all the things that you have done in their absence, even if you may be stretching the truth. They will soon get the idea that it is safe for them to go off and they don't need to keep an eye on you. When they behave really badly on their return it is easy to blame it on what has happened during contact. It is more likely that they are testing you to see if you will unconditionally love them despite them betraying you by seeing your ex. They will be marking their territory. They will need constant reassurance until they get the message that it is okay for them to go.

Ask them whether they have had a good time, take an interest in what they did. Make sure they feel that your questions aren't a way of spying on your ex but that you are genuinely interested in what they have done, much as you would if they had been with school friends or with their grandparents.

It is reassuring when your children can comfort you when you are sad about things and are sensitive to your moods. What is not good is when they assume the role of parent to you and you become the child to them. It is a world of upside down. To preserve your emotional well-being over contact, by all means communicate with your ex for a desired outcome; but know that, if you don't get the response you want, you need to look at whether it really does matter to you that much, and more importantly, whether it is harmful for your child.

A child and adolescent psychiatrist once said to me that, in the scheme of things, children aren't damaged by too many presents or going to bed late. No child grows up and says, I had too many presents when I was young and it has damaged me, or says, I went to bed too late when I was with my dad/mum and now look at me. What is damaging is neglect or abuse, and the conflict that they get caught up in. If the complaints you have don't come into that category, then free yourself of the tiring and tiresome wrangling that they cause. Obviously, you can't pretend to be totally unaffected – clock the complaints, communicate them in a measured way, but don't let them drag you into an exhausting and exhaustive place. This is your time. You have wonderful resources for improving and moving on with your life.

Children meeting new partners

Marta and Stefan had been divorced for a year. They had two children aged seven and five. When the children came back from seeing their dad, Marta was shocked to the core to hear them talking about a woman called Fay, who was 'really nice' and had played table tennis with them and taken them shopping. There had been no discussion between her and Stefan about introducing this new girlfriend to the children and Stefan didn't seem to understand why Marta was so upset. He said Fay was relaxed with the children and the children liked her, so what was the problem? What he hadn't even thought about was the impact on their mother and the feeling that any voice she might have had in the deci-sion making around it had been hijacked. He was really surprised at how she felt.

When should the children meet any new partner? If you are not the parent with the new partner, you will probably be saying never. You may well want to do all you can to ensure that there is no other 'parent' in the frame, fearful that your children might like them too much. You worry that your ex's new partner will assume the role of parent and usurp your authority and autonomy.

At the same time you will want the new partner to be nice so that your children are treated well if they have to meet him or her. You will want to buy time, to put the event off to some distant point in the future so that you can forget about it. It doesn't always work out this way.

Children will need to get used to their parents' separation before anyone else comes into the frame. They need to know in words but also to see that the parent who has moved out or the one who they see less often is there for them and fully available when they do see him or her.

Ideally, you and your ex should discuss the timing and process of the introduction and agree something that seems acceptable. It should then be done with care, explaining to the children beforehand that they are going to meet Daddy or Mummy's new friend. At first, it is best for them to spend short periods of time with the new partner, so that they can get used to him or her.

Importantly, if the new relationship does not look like it's going to be long term, it would be best to not bring the children into it. They don't need to be exposed to a constant stream of new parental partners. They will also need to see that their other parent is ok with the new relationship, so that they don't feel disloyal for accepting something that they have no choice over.

As far as you are concerned, there will never be a challenger for your children's affections. You are and always will be their parent, no matter how nice the new partner is to them.

Social media and children

Katya had an eight-year-old son. Her partner left her for someone else and she was devastated.

In anger, she took to Twitter, Facebook and Instagram to let the world know that she would not be 'beaten'; she would live to tell the tale and she and her son would be a team for ever. They would not let her ex bring her down. She posted pictures of them together and where they lived. People liked her posts and made disparaging comments about her ex to support her.

In the consulting room, she told me that she was waging war on him and he would not get away with it. She said that he had got away scot-free and was living the life of Riley. She said that by the time she was finished, no one would be fooled into thinking he was a good person. Katya hoped that their mutual friends would abandon him.

Katya believed that when 'justice' was done she would be free. Actually, the fight, played out through social media, imprisoned her, as she was using it to externalise everything, so that all the pain of her divorce was 'out there' rather than being digested internally. She was so caught up with the need for retribution that she didn't even give herself time to think about the impact it might have on her child at school or with his friends.

On social media, you can't always restrict who sees what, or shares what. Her son soon became the subject of gossip, the unwitting star of his own gritty soap opera, and everybody knew the family's business. It was very tough on him. There was nothing private left about his life and there was nowhere he could go to get away from it.

Through social media, Katya's private family troubles became public. For her, the separation became a matter of 'let the world see and to hell with the consequences'. Although, of course, she loved her son and pledged to do everything she could to protect him from his father's behaviour, she was inadvertently contributing to his distress.

Katya was an extreme case of what happens when you take to social media but the impact on children is the same: it doesn't protect them; it strips away their privacy. Child psychotherapists would say that it is imperative to protect children in order for them to develop into trusting independent adults; one step towards doing this is to allow them the privacy that they are entitled to.

The privilege of a lifetime is to become who you truly are.

Carl Jung

EXERCISES

Walking in your children's shoes exercise

Take a sheet of paper and a pen. Before you start, take stock for a minute and put yourself in the position of your child.

Write a list of what your child needs from you and your ex during this period of separation or post-separation – do this from your child's perspective, as if you *are* your child. Think about whether you are writing down what *you* think they need. If you are, stop and think about what *he* would write if he were writing the list. Remember: this is meant to be from his point of view.

- Take some time to do this rather than hurry.
- Then read it through.
- How does it make you feel?

Some people say this exercise makes them feel sad or guilty. It is not meant to do that and there is no need to feel that way.

The fact that you are even undertaking the exercise means that you are doing your best to do what is right for your child. So, quieten the critical voice and take something from it. It will give you a chance to put yourself in your child's shoes in order to put some perspective on the way you manage his experience of your separation.

Another question which is helpful to think about is: if you could fast-forward time so that your child is now an adult talking to a friend, what do you think he would say about his experience of the period of time around the separation?

The answer to that will give you a good indication of whether you are drawing him into things that shouldn't concern him or whether you are making the experience as good and positive as possible.

Just thinking about these questions will give you the opportunity to do things differently to make sure he has the best possible experience from now.

Self-esteem exercise

If you are feeling low and that life is moving on without you, I would like you to do this exercise.

Take a piece of paper and a pen. On the left-hand side of the page, make a list of words that you associate with low self-esteem. Take some time to do this, however painful it might be to think of those words.

Below are some of the feelings that people in my support groups have said they associate with low self-esteem:

- No confidence
- Feeling unattractive
- Feeling uncared for
- Left out
- Punished
- Cheated
- Colourless
- Rudderless
- Abandoned
- Different
- Failure

When you feel you have exhausted that list, make a

list on the right-hand side of the page of words that you associate with good self-esteem.

Here are some of the words that my groups have suggested:

- Empowered
- Grounded
- Confident
- Seeing the good in things
- Wise
- Empathetic
- Kinder
- Free of fear
- Hopeful
- In control

Look at the two lists and compare them.

The task for the next few days is to think about how you can move from the feelings and thoughts in the left-hand column to those on the right. What would it take, for example, to move from feeling rudderless to feeling grounded? Thinking about it brings the possibility of change.

There is something creative about moving the boundaries of your experience. Every so often come back to the thought of expanding your view so that it doesn't feel so confining. The act of thinking about it will start to shift your experience of it.

If that feels difficult, try and think about what it would take to open your mind to the possibility of change and movement. Look at the first column and realise that nothing in it is static or fixed; rather, it is the base for change. Just thinking about it will enable you to take the first steps.

Picturing yourself and your relationship exercise

This is an exercise I do with my groups. Often people say they can't draw but it really doesn't matter. This isn't an art competition, you may be talented but on the other hand what you produce may also be worthy of a 5-year-old and that is fine.

Take an A4 sheet of paper and turn it sideways. Draw a line down the middle.

On the left-hand side, draw a picture of yourself and your marriage. Try not to use words, just draw. You may be asking what I mean by a picture of you and your marriage: don't give it too much thought, just draw what comes to mind.

On the right-hand side of the paper, draw a picture of you and your life now. Again, try to just draw rather than adding any words. Interpret what is being asked of you in whatever way you want.

When you have finished it, have a good look at what you have drawn. At first it will just look like two pictures and you won't really know what you are looking for. Take a closer look.

There are all sorts of things that you may begin to notice.

Are you bigger in one than in the other? If you have children, where have you placed them in relation to yourself and your ex? In the marriage picture have you even included your ex? If you have, where is he or she standing in relation to you and/or your children? Have you drawn a house in either or both pictures? Does it have windows or a door? Have you drawn any facial features on the picture of yourself or your ex or your children? Are there features on some of them and not others? Have you drawn hands or feet?

All these observations will reveal something quite powerful because you haven't used words. Have you omitted to give yourself a mouth in the marriage side and yet given yourself one on the now side? That may tell you that you had no voice then but do have one now, which might surprise you. You might believe you still don't have a voice: the picture will be telling you that's not right. You may have drawn yourself bigger than your ex and yet you see yourself as small – another surprise. You might have drawn the children next to you and away from your ex, showing that in fact you think you have a stronger relationship with your children than he or she has. Are you floating in the air with your feet above the ground? This could mean that at the moment you don't feel grounded, or didn't then. If your house had no windows, perhaps your real feelings were that you were trapped then or that you had nothing to dream about as everything was all turned in on itself. That idea might challenge your belief that everything was rosy in your marriage.

The purpose of this exercise is to show you that there are things that you may not be fully aware of – about the past, the present and how far you've come. It is helpful to see things from a different perspective, one that you may not have thought of before. Drawing is a very effective way of putting you in touch with those aspects of yourself.

You may find it helpful to show your drawing to a friend and ask him or her to comment on what they see in it. Or, if you can, do the exercise with someone else who is either in the process of separation or already separated and then comment on each other's drawings.

Go back to your drawing after a few days; you will see other things then too.

Attributes exercise

Make a list of all the attributes and qualities you think you possess. Just managing, navigating and surviving your separation will have required all sorts of qualities – and that is without even thinking about all the other ones you draw on in your everyday life.

When you've finished, take a good look at the list. By looking at it you will see in black and white what at this stage can be hard for you to grasp. Being caught up in the distress of separation almost obliterates anything good. Making lists enables you to see for yourself that what your mind is telling you simply isn't true. You have depths and resources that you need to see plainly written on a page in order to start to believe in them.

The members of one of my support groups made the following list of their own qualities:

Driven
Not giving up
Believing in myself
Integrity
Courage
Strong
Principled

Amazing
Calm
Determination/conviction
Surviving
Unselfish
Giving
Self-respect
Proving
Truthful

Achievements exercise

Take some time to think about what you have achieved in your life. I know that your immediate response might be to think that there is very little to write down. That will just be a reflection of how you are feeling about yourself at the moment. Try to override that feeling and dig deep to get in touch with your achievements.

It could be something concrete, like academic or professional qualifications, jobs, or sporting achievements.

It could be simple: good cook, great dancer or passing your driving test. It could be just the act of staying in work despite the difficulties, or being a good parent in the face of provocation, or being a good friend to someone who needs you, or being a trusted member of your family. Whatever it is, it certainly isn't nothing.

So, get writing whatever comes to mind. Try to get to a list of 20.

There is no rush; you can do this over a period of time and keep revisiting it and adding to it. When you have finished, pin it up on the fridge or your bathroom mirror and look at it every so often.

Monitor how you feel now you have listed and recognised all your achievements.

The purpose of this exercise is to show you that you

are not unworthy or helpless; on the contrary, you have lived a life and are entitled to stand up and be recognised for what you've achieved.

Although your personal circumstances have changed, your achievements have not. Keep the list as a healthy reminder of that, and use it to change your perception of and your attitude to yourself.

Who am I exercise

In my support groups, people often say that they learn more about someone's ex-partner than they do about the person actually sitting in the group. Why is that? It is because people talk more about their ex than about themselves. If you talk mainly about your ex, you are giving him or her more importance than yourself. You are not doing yourself any favours with this; you are denying people the joy of getting to know you and you are devaluing yourself. Remember that it is *your* life and *you* that people want to get to know.

In a separation, it is often easy to lose sight of who you are. It feels as if your whole being is subsumed in the separation and its consequences. Perhaps during your marriage, you slowly forgot about the person that you were before you met your partner. Perhaps you don't know who you are any more and find it hard to think about, let alone get in touch with, the person you were before.

We give a lot of ourselves away in relationships. They change us; we become co-dependent, doing certain things whilst our partners do others. In that process, sometimes we can forget our own strengths, and lose abilities in certain areas, whether it's booking holidays or arranging the finances. The more dependent we are on others, the more we lose touch with our own capabilities. It doesn't mean we don't have those capabilities; we just feel that we don't.

Whilst it is very true that to get over something you need to talk about it until you can't talk about it any more, it is also important not to lose sight of something… and that something is *you*. This exercise is about *you*.

This is an exercise that illustrates the effect your separation has had on you and what you need to concentrate on, to make it stop defining you.

You can do it by yourself or with a friend.

If you are by yourself:
Really think hard about who you are. You may be an aunt or a sister or a brother or a father, a daughter or son, or a nephew or a cousin or a friend. You may work and make a valuable contribution. You have importance to others *and* you are your own person. Others rely on you – maybe children, or a relative, or a work colleague – so you know that you are needed. If you are relied on, or depended on, this is part of who you are.

As soon as you start to think about your ex or what you might have been if it wasn't for him or her – STOP. Start again, and try to concentrate on you.

If you are with a friend with whom you would normally talk about your ex:
Ask if she or he would mind you talking about who you

are. Then do just that. As soon as the conversation veers off the road – STOP. Get back on track.

If this exercise has been difficult, you may see, without having realised it till now, just how far you have moved from having a sense of yourself. Perhaps your grief and anger have been so all-encompassing that you have become lost.

If this has happened to you, then it is time to act.

To recap…

Make a real effort to reconnect. Tell yourself that for 30 minutes at a time (you decide how often) each day, you forbid yourself to think of your ex and, more importantly, to talk about her or him. Clock whether it is easy or hard and force yourself to get back on track every time you fall off it.

Make a list of who you think you are.

I am:
Witty, capable, courageous, a good friend, good father, good mother…

The harder you find this, the more important it is that you do it. If nothing else, it shows you how much the break-up has knocked you away from yourself.

Reconnecting with yourself is one very important step in regaining your self-confidence and self-esteem. It will help you find your place in your new world, a place that is comfortable and secure. It is a step, but certainly one in the right direction.

Rocky road exercise

- Take a sheet of paper and draw a road on it. Any road, bumpy or straight. This is the road of your divorce journey.
- Name the beginning of the road 'Separation'.
- Now give the end of your road a name, like 'Feeling Better' or 'Happiness' – a word or term that you will recognise as representing that the separation is behind you. You name it: it is your personal road.
- Make a cross on your road, to represent where you were emotionally at the beginning of your separation.
- Now make a cross showing where you feel you are on your road today.

Take a look: Are you surprised at what you see? Are your two crosses in different places on the road? Is the second one, which represents where you are now, further towards the feeling better end? Does it tell you something that you hadn't realised?

It is letting you know that things are changing even if you might have thought that they weren't. Even if there is a small gap between the two crosses there is movement and there will continue to be. Try to do this exercise once a month. It may surprise you.

If there is no movement, perhaps you are very newly separated. If not, you may need some outside help to explore why things don't seem to be changing – you may be stuck, and unable to move on. You *will* move but only when you are ready to and perhaps with some professional help. Can you think about what is stopping you from moving along the road? The 'Feeling stuck' and 'Letting go of grievance' chapters might help you with this.

Demonstrating how you feel symbolically, with a drawing rather than words, can be very powerful. This exercise can really have an impact on the way you see things, offering a visual representation of something you don't always allow yourself to believe, and showing you that things do shift, sometimes slowly and in tiny steps. But, with each small step, the trauma of your separation recedes further into the background, beginning to occupy a place of memory rather than tainting your view of the world.

Acknowledgements

Breaking Upwards might not have seen the light of day without the invaluable support and help of others. Thanks are due to: Cecily Engle for the introduction to Short Books, in particular thanks to Aurea Carpenter my editor and Rebecca Nicolson; Barnaby Spiro for conceiving its title; Olivia Lichtenstein who, having read the introduction all those months ago, told me to 'get on and write it'; also my thanks to Nick Hastings, Stephen Nathan QC, Susan Caplan, Lola Borg, Miranda and Isabelle Spiro; and to Arela Natas and David Morgan whose wise words enabled me to take the manuscript out of its dusty box and into the sunlight.

CHARLOTTE FRIEDMAN

is a psychotherapist working in central London. Having been a barrister for 25 years, specialising in divorce and separation, she retrained as a family therapist and now sees many couples and individuals going through the process. Charlotte has often appeared on TV and radio and presents workshops and seminars for many big companies.